CHAPTER 1: WHAT PRODUCTIVITY MEANS TO DIFFERENT PEOPLE

The word productivity means the same thing whatever way you look at it. It means getting more out of what you put into something. But the context in which that is done can make it mean different things to different people, including the following:

Reading the bedtime story

To a working parent, productivity can mean not having to sacrifice the bedtime story to do a good job ever again. It can mean always being there for your kids' birthday or sports day or school play or whatever occasion is important to them. Figuring out how to work flexibly and fit work around your life can help you have a great work-life balance and still do a top job.

Being first to market

For the start-up, productivity can be the difference between being first to market or fifth. The more effective methods you use to get the job done each day, the more quickly you can produce what you want to produce. Cutting-edge technology or scientific breakthrough all depend on the productivity of the people to get it to the masses as quickly as possible. Waste too much time on emails, and you may find yourself at the back of the queue for recognition.

Keeping the doors open

Increasing productivity can help to produce goods at a lower cost. If you're responsible for the wages of your employees, increased productivity can mean they get paid again this month. To a business owner, productivity, can mean keeping the doors open.

Making the grade and the party

To a student, productivity means making the grade and the party. A student wants to fit it all in – attend classes, go to the gym, have time to study, and still make it to all the best parties. These are the priorities of a student, and becoming more productive can make them a possibility.

What can productivity mean to your Business

People are generally more familiar with the business benefits of productivity – increased profits, competitiveness and less employee stress, to name but a few.

But businesses today are faced with increased competition from emerging markets along with a more demanding customer who wants it all and wants it now.

Forever under pressure to cut costs, and with the emerging war for talent, being in business is no walk in the park. Productivity is a powerful tool that can help you to address these challenges and give organi- sations a competitive edge. This section covers the benefits of productivity for businesses.

Making the difference between profit and loss:

Most people understand productivity in its traditional sense: increase productivity and experience greater profits. To a CEO, increased productivity can mean a good year. How this difference was made could be made up of a hundred different factors. Productivity could have been increased through changes in factory processes, through the influence of a new manager who helped all employees perform at their best or through the new computer system that cut out all the downtime.

The outcome is of most interest to the CEO, but his managers should know how to replicate the increase by understanding its source.

Reducing employee stress:

Increased productivity usually results in a reduction in stress. When people learn how to work more effectively and manage their time and energy better, they tend to benefit from a feeling of control and reduced stress.

This reduction in individual stress can have a positive impact on the people, their team and the whole organisation. Stress is responsible for so many negative factors in a working environment.

Being innovative:

Productive employees tend to have more time for strategic thinking time and innovation. Only when you're relaxed and in control of your day can you take the time to visualise something better. Productivity usually leads to a more innovative company culture when employees are praised for the time spent dreaming or thinking of better ways to do things.

When an organisation is under time pressure to achieve its daily goals, any time not spent on the core activities will generally be frowned upon. If a company doesn't take the time to innovate, its future won't be very bright.

Creating a culture of success:

Productive organisations are more successful. Their people tend to take the lead and tend to be more proactive, more creative and more innovative. They're generally people who take responsibility for their own actions and circumstances. This can result in a culture where people are more likely to think beyond the daily remit. They'll be more inclined to have ideas and be willing to share and follow up on them. Calm control breathes success.

CHAPTER 2:
DISCOVERING WHY PRODUCTIVITY MATTERS TO YOU

So, why do you want to get productive? Is it to increase your performance at work, to deliver more and do better? Or is it to have a better quality of life and improve your work-life balance and be happier? The following sections include some of the main reasons people want to improve their productivity.

Improving work-life balance

Probably one of the chief reasons people buy self-help books is to improve their work-life balance. They feel overwhelmed with too much to do or not enough time to spend with family or friends. Productivity and this book are the perfect solution for improving your work-life balance and figuring out what merits your time and attention. When you understand what is important to you in your life, you can work toward changing the things that need to be changed.

Reducing personal stress

Increased productivity usually results in a reduction in stress. When people figure out how to work more effectively and manage their time and energy better, they tend to benefit from a feeling of control and reduced stress. Feeling organized means you no longer have to worry about things you need to do or would like to do. You'll have a system to look after all of your tasks and dreams and goals. Taking charge will help you to feel like you're driving your life forward rather than being pulled in too many directions.

Doing a better job

Productive employees tend to have more time for strategic thinking time and innovation. Only when you're relaxed and in control of your day can you take the time to visualize something better. Productivity usually leads to more creativity, innovation and enhanced performance all around.

Making time for creativity

Many people think productivity and creativity are at opposite sides of the court. They think that organized, productive people aren't creative. This is not the case. The more productive I become, the more peaceful my mind becomes. If I have all the boring stuff organized and taken care of, I can free my mind to be more creative. Stress caused by disorganization will negatively affect creativity. Productivity paves the way for creativity to bloom. Chapters 8 and 12 have the de- tails on stimulating creativity.

Making time for strategic thinking

Many senior managers complain of not having enough time in their day. The problem is they prioritize badly, giving the daily tasks priority over the more important big-picture work. Managers need strategic thinking time. If you're disorganized and stressed with your workload, this time will rarely come. When you get organized and start to prioritize effectively, you'll have more time to focus on the important stuff like strategic thinking.

Improving your quality of life

Many things may need to change in your life, your relationships, your work or even the time you spend with yourself. Getting organized is a great first step to making changes in your life. Getting organized helps you to see clearly what you want from your life. When you have this clarity, you can introduce systems that will help you to achieve more order. With the right attitude and habits, you can maintain a relaxed, organized calm in all areas of your life.

CHAPTER 3: THE SCARCITY OF TIME

L isten in astonishment to the most severe examples on news broadcasts: stories involving someone who becomes so outraged over a seemingly trivial event that he assaults and injures or even kills another person. Road rage is one of the most common manifestations of this disorder, but there are many others and can involve almost any human activity. All that's required are two or more people, a spark, and a participant who takes the whole thing way too seriously. And it appears these ingredients are available and come into contact with each other with surprising frequency.

These are extreme manifestations of what is typically referred to as "hurry sickness," a state of anxiety caused by the feeling of not having enough time in the day to accomplish everything that is required. Some people are so intent upon achieving their goals, that any disruption, even the ordinary, everyday kind, can send them into a homicidal, unthinking rage.

We wonder how these people can lose control so quickly and completely, and are comforted knowing we are more rational, more balanced, and better adjusted. We are unaffected by minor interruptions, and are in complete control of our emotions and actions.

Are we, really? While most of us, thankfully, are not prepared to commit mayhem when things don't go our way, many of us have a serious problem dealing with events that knock us off course, interfering with our goals. We are a nation of overachievers, with lives stuck on fast forward.

With little time to plan, many of us have become adept at crisis management, rushing to put out one fire after another. We're all dependent on overnight delivery and communicating via e-mail, fax, and telephone. We're constantly connected by personal digital assistants and Phones, and we time our commitments to the minute so we can fit them into our crowded schedules.

Riding The Adrenaline High

Here's another simple test to diagnose a possible case of hurry sickness. Just respond "yes" or "no" to the following statement: "I work better under pressure."

A lot of us seem to think so. We claim the trait on our resumes (along with "highly motivated self-starter"), and we brag about our ability to perform under the tightest of deadlines.

Some of us pick up this habit in college, waiting to write that term paper until the day before it's due, pulling an all-nighter, and going to class bleary eyed, bedraggled, but smugly self-satisfied that another challenge has been successfully met. Knowing how clever we are, we carry over the habit to other areas of our lives and press forward confident and hopeful that others will recognize our talents as well.

You, too? Go back and look at that work after you've calmed down. Your best? If you're honest with yourself, you'll admit the quality of the work suffers when you race through it.

And you suffer, too. You've got motion sickness — not the kind that causes queasiness when you react to the rolling of a ship, but rather a physical and psychological dependence on motion and speed that can become almost as powerful as a true addiction.

"Leisure time" has become an oxymoron. We experience one long workday, broken but not relieved by gulped meals and troubled sleep. Only the models in the clothing catalogs seem to have time to lounge.

People take shorter and fewer vacations, and we take our work with us, with our beepers and cell phones, faxes and email. Our home computers are extensions of the office, but being able to work at home means we're always at work.

Leisure is not as leisurely as it once was, and we race through life checking the "fun" items off the to-do list.

Even our play has become purposeful with physical conditioning or enforced "relaxation," and competitive pastimes (who plays golf without keeping score?). Even birdwatching has become a competitive sport.

Simple Symptoms And Scary Consequences Of Hurry Sickness

How about you? Have you got a case of hurry sickness?

Symptoms include:

✓ Nervousness

✓ Depression

✓ Fatigue

✓ Appetite swings

✓ Compulsive behavior (repetitive actions that are difficult or even impossible to stop)

✓ Unwillingness and even inability to stop working

✓ Inability to relax even when you do stop working

That's not good, but it's not lethal. Hold on. It gets worse. We all have to run the occasional sprint, meet the unyielding deadline, cope with the unforeseen emergency. And we can do so effectively and without long-term damage. It can even be exhilarating. But keep driving in that fast lane until it becomes a way of life and you run the risk of:

✓ Hypertension

✓ Heart disease

✓ Migraines

✓ Insomnia

✓ Digestive problems

✓ Stroke

The stress of rushing through life suppresses the immune system, hampering the natural formation of T-lymphocytes (white blood cells) and leading to increased susceptibility to infection and cancer. Life in the fast lane can make you sick. It can even kill you.

Just What Is Time, Anyway?

Here's a simple way to find out what time is to you. Jot down several phrases that use the word "time" in them.

Make them descriptive of the way you relate to time. For example, you might write:

"I'm trying to learn to spend my time wisely," or

"I've found that I can save time by making a to-do list every morning before work," or

"I tend to waste time after dinner."

Now rewrite each statement, but substitute the word "life" for the word "time" and see what you come up with. In our examples above, we'd get:

"I'm trying to learn to spend my life wisely."

"I've found that I can save my life by making a to-do list."

"I tend to waste my life after dinner."

The point to this little parlor trick? (Did you think of it as a "waste of time"?) If even one of your revised statements startled you, even a little bit, you got the point. We aren't talking about some tangible commodity when we discuss the time of our lives. We're talking about our very lives.

We no more "have" time than we "have" inches of height.

Time is nothing more (or less) than a way of measuring out our lives. Other cultures measure time in other ways, and some cultures don't measure it at all.

Here are how some other cultures speak of time:

"Think of many things. Do one." — Portuguese saying

"Sleep faster. We need the pillows." — Yiddish saying

"Haste has no blessing." — Swahili saying

"There is no hand to catch time." — Bengali saying

"Today can't catch tomorrow." — Jamaican saying

That's not to say we shouldn't learn from the past and plan for the future, even if we can't store it or hold it.

We're going to do a great deal of learning and planning as we explore time together. However, although we remember the past and envision the future (both highly creative acts), we can't live in either one of them.

You can use this basic checklist, four questions to help you make those decisions:

✓ What has to be done?

✓ What has to be done first (what's most important)?

✓ How much of it has to be done?

✓ How fast does it have to be done (what's the deadline)?

The answers to these questions will enable you to decide what to do now. These decisions will add up to your whole life being well lived.

CHAPTER 4: THE IMPORTANCE OF TIME MANAGEMENT

B ecause you have only 24 hours in each and every day, making the best use of these hours makes good sense. Once those hours have gone you can't get them back, and you can't make more of them if you lose or waste them. They're a finite resource, which means spending a little time brushing up your time management skills can transform your life in various ways.

Increasing productivity

It's all too easy to get to the end of the day and wonder what you've actually achieved, even though you feel as though you haven't stopped all day. Many a time I've known people who say, 'I've been really busy all day, but what did I do?' I've done it myself. You're busy, but not necessarily productive.

Managing your time means you're more effective. You get more done in less time, you focus on the important things and so your overall productivity increases.

For example, by managing your time better, you may be able to carve out an extra half-hour a day. Spend that half-hour on your most important project every day for a week and you'll be astonished at how you chip away at the work. Good time management now has a great long-term effect.

Reducing stress

If I were to wave a magic wand and give you an extra hour in every day, what would you do? Usually when I ask this question, the most common responses are sleep and exercise, or just time to relax. These responses go to show what kind of activities tend to get pushed to one side when time is short or when people try to cram too much into what's available and what's physically possible.

You get caught in a vicious circle. You never get time to catch up or get on top of things. You just keep doing things the same way because you don't know how to do them any differently, or you feel that you just don't have the time. Eventually, something has to give and too often it's your physical and emotional health that suffers.

Developing better time management skills can reduce your stress levels. You're then able to manage your workload better and take control of your life rather than feel your life is controlling you all the time.

Achieving a happy work–life balance

The point of better time management is that you're able to do the things that are important to you and As working hours increase and people work longer and longer, getting some balance between your work life and your personal life becomes very important. If you didn't have work, you'd still have your family, friends, and your health. Developing better time management skills means you stop neglecting yourself and your loved ones because you're 'too busy at work'.

Managing your time effectively means you focus on what's important in the time you have available, so you make time for the essential things in life.

<u>Overcoming Obstacles</u>

Anyone can conquer time management, but it's not always easy. If your experience is anything like mine, sometimes your days feel like a video game, where you're in constant threat of being gobbled up on your course to the finish line. But instead of cartoon threats, your obstacles are your own shortcomings (poor communication skills, procrastination, and the inability to make wise and quick decisions), time-wasting co-workers and bosses, phone and people interruptions, and unproductive meetings.

Communicating effectively

Communicating effectively is one of the best ways to maximize your time.

One of the biggest time-wasters on company time is, no surprise, talking with co- workers. But what may be a surprise is that the abuse isn't a function of weekend catch-up discussions that take place at the water cooler or the gossip circle at the copy machine. Rather, it's the banter at the weekly staff status reports, the drawn-out updates of projects that never seem to conclude, and the sales presentations that get off-track. It's all the meetings that could be as brief as 10 minutes, but somehow take an hour or more.

At your disposal, however, is an amazing weapon for taming these misbehaving encounters: your words. With a few deft remarks, you have the power to bring these meetings to a productive close.

Circumventing interruptions

Interruptions creep into your workday in all sorts of insidious manners. Besides the pesky co-worker stepping into your office with "Got a sec?" interruptions come in the form of unproductive meetings, phone calls, hall conversations that drift into your office and distract you, even the "you've got mail" icon that creeps onto the lower corner of your computer monitor.

Additionally, most poor time managers interrupt themselves by trying to do too much at once. Study after study supports that multitasking isn't the most effective work style. The constant stops and starts disrupt a project, requiring startup time each time you turn back to the task.

Getting procrastination under control

Sometimes, it's tempting to use interruptions as an excuse to postpone a project or a task. How nice to have someone else to blame for not getting started! And before you know it, you've found so many good reasons not to do something that you've backed yourself into a really tight eleventh-hour corner, and the pressure's on.

Procrastination has a lot of causes, but most of the reasons to procrastinate leave you headed for trouble.

CHAPTER 5: PUTTING A VALUE ON YOUR TIME

Depending on your values, different kinds of numbers may be important to you: To some, it's cholesterol count and blood pressure figures; to others, it's the number of years they've been married. To many, the sum total in the retirement account is the number-one number, and some people zero in on the amount left on their mortgage.

But I contend that your per-hour worth should be among the top-of-mind numbers that are important to you no matter what your values or priorities are — even if you don't earn your living on a per-hour rate.

Knowing the value of your time enables you to make wise decisions about where and how you spend it so you can make the most of this limited resource according to your circumstances, goals, and interests.

Obviously, the higher you raise your per-hour worth while upholding your priorities, the more you can propel your efforts toward meeting your goals, because you have more resources at your disposal — you have either more money or more time, whichever you need most.

Getting a Good Grip on the Time-Equals- Money Concept Your per-hour value translates to your quality of life, both now and in the future. Not only does your income influence how you spend your nonworking hours, but it also determines how much leisure time you have to spend.

As you can imagine, your hourly value reaches beyond the basics: It impacts your health, too. For instance, studies show that lower-income earners have more health problems, including heart disease and diabetes, which are often attributed to poor diets and a lack of medical care. Additionally, the challenge of trying to make ends meet can cause great stress, leading not just to physical illness but also to depression and other mental health problems.

And though it's important to live in the present, it's also important to keep an eye toward the future. How well you prepare does have an impact on your quality of life right now. Making enough money to be able to save for retirement and other major life expenses including a child's education — results in a sense of comfort and safety about your future.

Your personal time has value, too. And by having a grip on the value of your work hours, you gain a better grasp on what your downtime is worth. After all, most people work so they can make the most of their personal time, whether they're devoting it to family, hobbies, volunteer work, travel, or education. You gain the perspective you need to make choices:

1. Is the extra money you'll gain by working overtime worth giving up your holiday with your family?

2. Could you work part-time and stay at home with your small children?

3. Can you afford to take a leave of absence to do a volunteer stint in Haiti?

4. Should you take on a freelance project that means giving up all your free time for three months to fund your dream trip to Bali?

5. But what is an hour of your personal time worth?

Calculating Your Hourly Income

No matter your occupation, everyone sells time for a price; it's just a lot more transparent in some situations than others. Most obvious are individuals who receive a wage or a fee based on the hours they work, including minimum-wage workers and self-employed individuals such as tutors, house cleaners, and consultants.

Other people advertise their prices based on a per-project basis, but in reality base that fee on an estimate of project hours the job takes. Freelance writers, for instance, may charge $1,500 to write a promotional brochure, but that amount is likely a reflection of the writer's value of his or her time at a certain figure — say, $75 per hour.

Some businesses and professions charge customers based on an hourly rate, although workers don't directly receive that per-hour fee. Instead, their salary or compensation is based on the revenue the company can bring in based on those hours. Law firms and plumbers, for example, may charge for their services on an hourly basis and pay their employees a salary or a per-hour rate.

Calculate the number of hours you work per week.

Work hours/day × days/week + overtime = hours/week

To be completely accurate, calculate your hourly rate based on the hours you actually work. If you consistently put in more than 40 hours a week (most salaried folks aren't paid overtime for additional hours worked), add those hours to your total. Here's an example:

8 hours/day × 5 days/week + 2 hours overtime = 42 hours/week

Figure out how many hours you work per year.

Work hours/week × weeks/year = hours/year

Make sure you subtract time off. For instance, if you take three weeks of vacation each year, subtract that from your total number of weeks worked. If your salary is based on a three-week vacation and an average 42-hour work week, here's how many hours you work per year:

42 hours/week × 49 weeks/year = 2,058 hours/year

Divide your gross salary by the number of hours you work per year.

Salary ÷ hours/year = hourly income

For instance, $80,000 divided by 2,058 hours is $38.87.

Boosting Your Hourly Value through Your Work Efforts

Most people think if they work more hours, they'll automatically make more money. That's faulty thinking: You can devote more hours to work, but if you invest the hours in the wrong actions, you gain nothing — and you lose time.

The solution may be to ask more money for your time. Some workers have a good deal of control over their hourly income and can therefore charge more per hour for their services. The freelance writer can raise her hourly rate from

$65 to $70 and bring in an additional $50 on a 10-hour project. A tax accountant can increase the fee for income tax preparation from $450 to $510. If he needs six hours to prepare the average income tax return, the accountant just gave himself an increase from $75 to $85 an hour.

However, the simple fact is that most people don't have the luxury of raising their income at will. So what's the next best step? Change how you use your time so you get the best return on investment — after all, what you do with your time leads to greater prosperity.

To increase your hourly value, you have to decide whether you'll work toward earning more money or earning more time. Then focus on performing high- value activities to achieve that goal; the process of discovering the really important actions or items you can invest your time in can help you change your hourly rate. The decision of how to increase your hourly value — whether to work toward generating more money in the same amount of time or generating the same amount of money in less time depends on your circumstances:

If you're in a commission or bonus compensation structure, you can increase productivity to earn additional income.

If you're in a salary-based position, you can find ways to be more productive within the 40 hours week and reduce the additional hours you put in.

Making Value-Based Time Decisions in Your Personal Life

When you consider the way you live your personal life, divide your focus in two: chores/responsibilities and leisure time. Although personal time may seem straightforward, there really is a difference between chores and leisure activities, and the way you approach your time-management decisions hinges on that difference. But however you spend your personal time, you can assign that time a value equal to your work worth — even though no one's paying you — to help you decide how to spend it.

Deciding whether to buy time: Chores and responsibilities

When you have a handle on the value of your time in hourly increments (see the earlier section "Calculating Your Hourly Income"), you have the information you need to make better time choices. The chores have to be done, whether you do them, or delegate, or even pay someone else to do them. The question with chores is whether you want to do them yourself or to exchange dollars for someone else to do them.

You have to ask, "Is the cost of the time this task would take me greater than or less than the cost to hire someone to do the work?" Here, you're simply com- paring numbers. Think of the laundry list of household chores and personal errands that can eat up every bit of personal time you have. If you could pay someone to do some of those tasks at a rate equal to or well below your hourly rate, wouldn't that be a good return on your investment?

For example, paying $50 to have your grass cut each week may have been a cost barrier you couldn't get over before. But if you've determined that the hourly value of your time is $50 per hour and it takes you 3 hours to mow your lawn, you've just bought yourself $100 worth of time ($150 worth of your time minus $50 to outsource the work). On the other hand, if you have all kinds of free time on the weekend — and you enjoy being out in the yard — paying someone else to cut your grass may be a money-time trade that has no value for you.

If you love to garden but hate cleaning the house, and cleaning the house takes you 4 hours ($200 if your time is worth $50 per hour), why not pay a house cleaning service $70, $80, even $100 to buy back the four hours it'd take you to do it all? And you buy yourself four blissful hours puttering over your zinnias and scarlet runner beans.

CHAPTER 6: THE SPECIFICS OF DAILY PRIORITIZATION

After you identify the vital few tasks you need to accomplish to meet your top 12 goals, break them down a bit further into daily to-do items. Then prioritize them to make sure you accomplish the most important tasks first, identifying which ones you must do on a given day.

In that way, you progressively work through all the minor tasks that lead to the greater steps that, in time, lead you to achieving your goals. Here's how:

Start with a master list.

Write down everything you need to accomplish today. Don't try ranking the items at this point. You merely want to brain dump all the to-do actions you can think of. You may end up with 20, 30, even 50 items on your list: tasks as mundane as checking e-mail and as critical as presenting a new product marketing plan to the executive board. Or if you want to fill work on your personal to-do list, the items may range from buying cat food to filing taxes before midnight.

Remember to account for routine duties that don't have a direct effect on your company's mission or bottom line: turning in business expense reports, typing up and distributing meeting minutes, taking sales calls from prospective printing vendors.

Neglecting to schedule the humdrum to-do items creates a destructive domino dynamic that can topple your well-intentioned time-block schedule.

Determine the A-list.

Focusing on consequences creates an urgency factor so you can better use your time. Ask yourself, "What, if not done today, will lead to a significant consequence?" Designate these as A activities. If you have a scheduled presentation today, then that task definitely hits the A-list. Same goes for filing your tax return if the date is April 15. Buying cat food probably doesn't make this list — unless you're totally out or have a particularly vindictive cat.

Categorize the rest of the tasks.

Now move on to B-level tasks, activities that may have a mildly negative consequence if not completed today. C tasks have no penalty if not completed today, followed by D tasks: D is for delegate.

These are actions someone else can take on. Finally, E items are tasks that could be eliminated, so don't even bother writing an E next to them — just mark them out completely.

Rank the tasks within each category.

Say you've categorized your list into six A items, four B items, three C items, and two D items. Your six A tasks obviously move to the top of the list, but now you have to rank these six items in order: A-1, A-2, A-3, and so forth.

If you have trouble ordering several top priorities, start with just two: Weigh them against each other — if you could complete only one task today, which of the two is most critical? Which of the two best serves your 80/20 rule? Then take the winner of that contest and compare it to the next A item, and so on. Then do the same for the B and C items.

As for the D actions? Delegate them to someone else! Everyone likes to think they're indispensable, but for most people, the majority of their duties could be handled by someone else. That's where the 85/10/5 rule — first cousin to the 80/20 rule comes into play: You tend to invest 85 percent of your time doing tasks that anyone else could do, and 10 percent of your time is devoted to actions that some people could handle. Just 5 percent of your energy goes to work that only you can accomplish.

But whether at home or at work, this doesn't mean you can kick back and leave 95 percent of your responsibilities to someone else. It simply helps you home in on the critical 5 percent, allocate your remaining time to other activities that bring you the greatest satisfaction, and recognize those tasks that are easiest to delegate.

Blocking off Time and Pluggin in To-Do Items

After you identify and order your priorities, you place them into time slots on your weekly calendar, broken into 15-minute segments, this process is commonly called time-blocking.

Like exercise, time-blocking can be tricky because it re- quires a lot of thought and adjustment, both in the initial stage where you're doing it for the first time and for a while thereafter, when you're developing the skill. Everybody knows what day two after the beginning of a new fitness program feels like: Stiff joints and sore muscles have you moving like the Tin Man after a rainstorm. At first you may feel like you'll never achieve the goals you've set, but sticking to the daily program eventually brings the results you want. Figuring out how to best manage your time depends on two things:

Consistent, diligent practice: If you want to build those time-blocking muscles, not only do you have to work them regularly, but you also need to in- crease the weight, stress, and pressure as you progress. Understanding the key to managing your minutes, hours, days, weeks, and so on takes repetition.

A span of time to improve: Achieving a level of time-blocking mastery does take time — a minimum of 18 months and as much as 24 months.

Implementing time-blocking to help organize your schedule takes a bit of time, but you reap huge dividends on that initial investment. This section walks you through a general outline of the process to follow.

Dividing your day

To start, you need a daily calendar divided into 15-minute increments. Why such small bites of time? Because even 15 minutes can represent a good chunk of productive activity. Losing just two or three of these small blocks each day can diminish your ability to meet your goals, from finishing that project at work to writing your best-selling (you hope) memoir.

On that blank schedule, begin by dividing your day; draw a clear line between personal time and work time. When you take this step, you're creating work-life balance from the start. Don't take it for granted that

Saturday and Sunday are time off just because you work a Monday through-Friday work week. Block it into your schedule, or work activities may creep into your precious downtime. The more you take action on paper, the more concrete the time-block schedule becomes.

Apprehensive about drawing a line between work and personal time because you're wary of having to tell a business associate you can't attend a business function that extends into personal time? Not to worry. You don't have to tell a client your Tuesday-morning workout is more important than a breakfast meeting with her, simply say you're already booked at that time. That's all the explanation you owe, and my experience shows that professional colleagues who want to do business with you will respect your boundaries.

Scheduling your personal activities

Blocking out personal activities first gives weight to these activities and ensures they won't be overtaken by obligations that have lesser importance in the long run.

Personal obligations are almost always the first thing most people trade for work; because of that, I recommend you hold fast and tight to the personal area so it doesn't get away from you. Another advantage?

Scheduling personal activities is twofold:

Schedule routine activities you participate in.

Do you have dinner together as a family every night? A weekly date night with your significant other? Do you want to establish family traditions? Don't just assume these activities will happen — give them the weight they deserve and block out the time for each one. Don't forget to include your extracurricular activities here: All those PTA groups, fundraising committees, nonprofit boards, and other volunteer commitments get plugged in as well.

Schedule personal priorities that aren't routine. Put those personal agenda items first before filling in your day with tasks and activities that don't support those priorities.

Factoring in your work activities

Begin with the activities that are a regular part of your job and then factor in the priorities that aren't routine. Whether you're a company CEO, a department manager, a sales associate, an administrative assistant, or an entry-level trainee, you're responsible for performing key tasks and activities each day and week. They may include daily or weekly meetings. Or maybe your responsibility is scheduling meetings for others. You likely have to prepare for these appointments. Perhaps you have to write and turn in reports or sales figures on an ongoing basis.

You may have to call someone for information routinely.

If you report to work daily and always spend the first hour of your day returning phone calls, time-block it into your schedule.

Accounting for weekly self- evaluation and planning time

Your goals — whether a one-year business plan or long- range retirement vision — warrant routine checkups.

Consider them as rest stops on your journey: Are you still on the right road? Is a detour ahead? Have you discovered a more direct route?

Use weekly strategic planning sessions — ideally for Friday afternoon or the end of the work week — to review your progress toward those near-future business projects as well as your larger career aspirations or personal goals. This is an opportunity to review the previous week and jump-start the upcoming week. I recommend spending 15 to 30 minutes daily and then taking a 90-to-120-minute session on self-evaluation and planning at the end of the week.

Building in flex time

Plug segments of time into your schedule every few hours to help you to minimize the fallout from unplanned interruptions or problems. About 15 or 30 minutes is enough time to work in at strategic intervals throughout your day. Knowing you have this free block of time can help you adhere to your schedule rather than get off track.

As you begin to build your time-blocking skills, insert 30-minute flex periods into your schedule for every two hours of time-blocked activity. This may seem like a lot of flex time, but if it allows you to maintain the rest of your time-block schedule and maintain or increase your productivity, it's worth the investment. My experience is the best time for flex time is after you've put in a couple of hours of your most important work — whether sales calls, report-preparation, or meeting a deadline.

Don't schedule flex time right before you go into an important activity time: You're more likely to get distracted and fail to get started with your critical business. Schedule it after the work — then you can use it, if necessary, to resolve any unforeseen problems.

Assessing Your Progress and Adjusting Your Plan as Needed

Becoming comfortable with time-blocking takes time, and achieving a glitch-free schedule that you can work with for a stretch may take a half-dozen revisions. Even then, routinely evaluate your time-blocking efforts and adjust them periodically to make sure you're getting the desired results. It's not a huge time investment — you can check yourself with a few minutes a day or use 15 to 30 minutes of your weekly time to review your results.

Ask yourself the following:

- ✓ What took you off track this week?
- ✓ What interruptions really affected your success with your time?
- ✓ Is someone sabotaging your time-block?
- ✓ What shifts would help your efficiency?
- ✓ In this section, I discuss this review in detail.

Surveying your results

One way to determine your effectiveness at time-blocking is to check results. In as little as two weeks from when you launch your time-blocking schedule, you can probably see where you need minor adjustments. The best way to keep tabs on results is to track them on an ongoing basis. I suggest both a weekly review that focuses on the past week and a periodic review of where you stand in relation to your overall goals.

The weekly review is a time for you to replay the tape of the week, looking at the highs and lows. I guarantee you'll have days where you want to pull your hair out because you face so many problems and distractions.

You'll also have days that are smooth as silk. What were the differences in those days besides the outcome?

As for the periodic review, review your job description, key responsibilities, and the ways in which your performance and success are measured. Then ask yourself these questions:

✓ Are you moving closer toward achieving your goals?

✓ Can you see measurable progress in reasonable time?

✓ Are you monitoring your performance well enough to see improvement?

✓ What changes do you need to adopt now to increase your speed toward reaching the goal and reduce the overall amount of time you invest?

Your success in meeting your objectives tells you whether the time-blocking is working for you.

Looking at measurable goals

If you can measure your goals in terms of numbers (dollars or sales, for example), then checking your results is a cinch. As a salesperson, for example, you may follow your sales numbers or commissions results over several months in order to get a good understanding of the effectiveness of your time-blocking efforts.

Or say you're a magazine editor who's evaluated on consistently meet- ing weekly publication deadlines; if your goal is to publish three articles per month in national magazines, you can assume your time-blocking efforts require some tweaking if your review reveals you're getting only one story in print.

CHAPTER 7: MATCHING TIME INVESTMENT TO RETURN

G enerally speaking, only 20 percent of those things that you spend your time doing produces 80 percent of the results that you want to achieve. This principle applies to virtually every situation in which you have to budget your time in order to get things done — whether at work, at home, in your relationships, and so on.

Sizing up your current situation

Before you can do any sort of strategizing, you need to take a good, honest look at how you use your time. For people who struggle with time management, the problem, by and large, lies in the crucial steps of assessing and planning. Start your assessment with these steps:

Observe how you currently use your time. Through the observation process, you can discover behaviors, habits, and skill sets that both negatively and positively affect your productivity. What do you spend most of your day doing? How far down the daily to-do list do you get each day?

Assess your personal productivity trends. During which segments of the day are your energy levels the highest? Which personal habits cause you to adjust your plans for the day?

Take a close look at the interruptions you face on a regular basis. During what segments of the day do you experience the most interruptions? What sort of interruptions do you receive most frequently, and from whom?

Identifying the top tasks that support your goals

Some folks tend to follow the squeeze-it-in philosophy:

They cram in everything they possibly can — and then some. These people almost always end up miserable be- cause they try to do so much that they don't take care of their basic needs and end up strung out in every possible way. The quality of what they do, as well as the amount of what they do, suffers as a result of their ever increasing exhaustion.

To work efficiently, you need to identify your 80 percent results you want to achieve. Take a good look at your top 12 goals and identify the tasks you need to do that align with those goals. If your number-one goal is to provide your kids with an Ivy League education, for example, then your priorities are less likely to center around taking twice-yearly vacations to the Caribbean and more likely to revolve around investing wisely and encouraging your offspring to do well in school (can you say "full-ride scholarship?").

After you identify what you need to do, spend a bit more time in self-reflection to double- check that you've correctly identified your goals and essential tasks. One of the biggest wastes of time for people is changing direction, priorities, objectives, and goals. Successful people and successful time managers take the direct route from point A to point B.

Here's what to ask yourself about these key tasks:

- ✓ How much time do you devote to those activities?
- ✓ Twenty percent? Less? More?
- ✓ What are you doing with the remainder of your time?
- ✓ How much return are you getting for the investment on the remainder?

Prioritizing your daily objectives

After you identify the tasks and activities that you need to accomplish to achieve your goals, assign a value to those goals so you can decide how to order your daily task list.

Take the send-your-kids-to-an-Ivy-League school scenario that I bring up in the preceding section: Even though another of your priorities is to be home for your kids, you as a nonworking parent who values the type of education you can provide for your 3-going-on-18-year-old more than the short-term joy of being a stay-at-home parent may decide to return to the workforce as you see tuitions skyrocketing. You can make this decision because you have a clear idea about how you rank your priorities. This clarity may help direct you to a job with hours compatible with your kid's schedule.

To personalize how you prioritize your goals at work, follow these steps:

Look at your long-term career goals.

Do you want to advance to a particular career level?

Do you want to achieve a particular income? Or is your goal to fine-tune your skill set before figuring out where you want to go next?

CHAPTER 8: SETTING UP AND MAINTAINING A PRODUCTIVE WORKSPACE

One study I saw indicated most people waste an hour per day trying to find papers lost on their desks (at least, that's where they think the papers are lost). That's not so bad, you say. But an hour per day adds up to 250 work hours per year, or more than 31 wasted days per worker annually.

Multiply that by the number of executives, professionals, and sales and administrative employees in this country, and you're talking a significant loss of time. (And that doesn't include hours spent at home trying to find misplaced eyeglasses, scissors, library books, keys, needle-nose pliers, cellphones, gym shorts, earrings, pacifiers, and so on.) Think how productive you'd be if you spent all that time, well, being productive!

Streamlining Your Workspace

"Don't touch my desk! I know exactly where everything is." I've heard that line endlessly, and I've used it myself. If you're like me, however, most of the time, as you stare at the forest of papers on your desk, you are clueless. You may have known where that phone number was yesterday, a few weeks ago, a month ago — or even a few minutes ago, but more stacks have since been added to the mix.

It's not enough to know which chart, report, or snippet of paper is on which pile, whether it's on the left or right side of your desk, or whether it's stashed in the catch-all drawer of your filing cabinet. This is your career you're talking about. Get a handle on it!

Make way! Clearing off your desk

Repeat after me: My desk is not a parking lot. My desk is not a parking lot. My desk is not a parking lot. If you want to get your desk under control, remember: Less is more. The more pictures, notes, boxes, tools (staplers, paper-clip holders, books), and so on that occupy your desk, the greater your odds of being distracted and the more cluttered your desk feels.

You also have less room to spread out if you're consulting multiple sources of information, using a laptop in addition to your desktop computer, or studying oversized charts or graphs. What's more, a topsy-turvy desk translates into greater stress and the misleading feeling you have all the time in the world to complete your projects.

Remove everything that isn't absolutely necessary from your desk. Be brutal. Here are some ideas to get you started:

1. Move family photos to your credenza or bookcase, where you can still see them throughout the day (and remember why you're working so hard) with- out their distracting you.

2. If you have other pictures — perhaps of you with mentors or celebrities — hang them on the wall.

3. Store extra tools, supplies, and items you use weekly in desk drawers and filing areas.

4. Don't allow items you rarely use or haven't looked at since slipping them into a pile to take up desk space. Put those items away in a filing cabinet, storage box, closet, or other less-accessible area.

As for your workspace, forget the Boy Scout be prepared motto. It's a recipe for desktop disaster, especially if you're one who likes to prepare for a flood, earthquake, alien invasion, and every other conceivable catastrophe.

The cleaner and clearer your desk, the better you can use your time.

Assembling essential organizational tools

Having the right tools for the job is really the start of great organization. If you haven't already done so, get all piles off your desk, even if you have to put them temporarily on the floor. Then gather these tools:

A desk organizer: You need some way to keep the standard office fare — staplers, paper clips, pens, calculators — handy at your fingertips.

Inboxes and outboxes: You need some type of organizational flow to your work that's based on an in-and-out system. Too often, interruptions happen when someone drops off something you don't need right now or stops by to pick something up. Setting up inboxes and outboxes outside the door of your office or cubicle keeps your desk clear and reduces chitchat.

A quality filing cabinet with space for growth: You may be surprised at how much filing space you need if you're a piler-turned-filer. I prefer lateral filing cabinets: They're more costly but can save a lot of time because you can see all the files at once.

Colored file folders: Ban bland manila! I suggest using the rainbow of colored folders available today. Consider a color-coded filing system, such as a stoplight approach with green for new business and other money-generating items, red for problem issues or customers, and so on. I also find that colors jog my memory when it comes time to find the files.

File folder labels: Labeling files is paramount to organization, efficiency, and time savings, even if you use colored folders. Labels can also be color-coded to further differentiate one file from another.

Setting up a timely filing system

Before you start going through papers, think about how you're most likely to search for the documents you need.

You can choose from numerous file-labeling strategies, but here are some possible categories:

- ✓ Customers (alphabetically)
- ✓ Past clients you no longer serve
- ✓ Due dates and project timing
- ✓ Pending projects
- ✓ On-hold projects

✓   To-dos, miscellaneous, or a similar catch-all type of label

You can choose to file by subject, client name, importance, or a number of other ways, but if time is of the essence, setting up a tickler filing system may be ideal. Tickler or reminder files have been around for ages. They make sure you remember to deal with delayed or deferred items at the correct times.

Here's how they work:

1. Establish two complementary tickler files, one labeled monthly and the other labeled daily.

    Your monthly tickler can be as simple as a 12-slot expandable folder with the months written onto each slot.

    Your daily tickler can be a 31-slot accordion file folder or even 31 hanging file folders, each labeled with dates 1 through 31.

2. As you receive new documents, place them in the appropriate slots of your monthly files.

    If a document you receive in December requires no action until March, place the document in the March slot of your monthly tickler file.

Tackling piles systematically

To de-clutter yourself, you need to remember this simple rule: Put the important things where you can remember where they are and where you can get to them quickly.

Here's how the decluttering process breaks down:

Figure out what you can get rid of.

Here are a few simple questions to ask yourself:

✓   Do you really need this? Really?

✓   Is there value in saving this item? (If the answer isn't a definitive yes, toss it.)

✓   What happens if you don't keep this?

✓   What's the worst that could happen if you throw this away?

Before you toss, think carefully about whether an item has future value and whether copies are filed elsewhere so you can access them if you need to.

Condense the offending material into smaller piles by selecting items to go into a single master important pile.

Many piles are simply files in disguise: Documents that haven't been put away where they belong. By collecting the most important items into a single pile, you get an idea of how much time you need to dissolve this pile into nothing.

At first, you may not be able to do much more than create your master important pile. After all, you stil have meetings to attend, e-mails to respond to, and work to finish. However, the master file ensures that you tackle the important stuff first; the smaller, less-important items have to wait.

Schedule an appointment with yourself in the next 48 hours to rid yourself of your master important pile.

You don't need to be in tip-top mental form to file. I suggest setting your filing appointment toward the end of the week, preferably in late afternoon when your energy level is low. Friday afternoons are a good time to file with comparatively few interruptions.

After making your master important file disappear, go back to your remaining clutter and repeat the process.

Start a second most-important master file and move all most-important items into that pile; then file them. Then make a third most-important master file.

By now, you can probably see the surface of your desk, and you may even have a substantial area cleared.

Keeping Clutter from Coming Back

Not so long ago, a handshake or verbal agreement sealed the deal. No more. Today, you need paper to confirm an agreement, assure mutual understanding, and even organize tasks. Paper has taken over people's lives.

Whether you're at home or at the office, maximizing your time means that all paper has to quickly find its way to the proper place, even if that place is the recycle bin or shredder. The key to controlling paper before it controls you is to decide quickly where to put it.

The best strategy for maintaining a clutter-free workspace is to avoid creating piles in the first place. You need to be more strategic in your work time to circumvent pile explosion. This section gives you two quick starts to circumvent the explosive growth of piles on your desk (or credenza, bookshelves, filing cabinets, extra chairs, window ledges, floor, or any other flat surface).

Handling papers once

Those who master paper have mastered single-handling.

These people touch a paper and take action. They don't pile, table, ponder, check, reconsider, or delay. They get rid of the paper the first time they handle it.

If you want to become a single handler, follow the five Ds: dump, delegate, detour, do it, or depot. Otherwise, you confront a less-productive list of Ds: dawdle, daydream, deliberate, and deceive — all of which lead to your demise.

Dump it

The dump-it principle is simple: Do you need it? If you don't, dump it or dispose of it. Say no to any of the following questions, and you can feel comfortable sending it to the shredder or recycling bin:

- Do you really need to act on this or keep it?
- Is this new, relevant information you need now or in the future?
- Does this information benefit a colleague or client?
- Are there consequences for not keeping it?
- Will this increase revenue or customer service?

Sort your mail over the recycling bin or waste basket. Everything that swirls into the bin or basket is no longer your problem.

Delegate it

Do you have an inner pack rat that wants to hold onto everything, including every paper that crosses your desk?

One way to shut down this impulse is to delegate papers to someone else. Even if you know you could complete the task with two hands tied behind your back, that doesn't mean it's the best use of your time. Delegate and give yourself more time to work on high-value tasks while building the skills and confidence of people you delegate to.

Detour it

Handling every sheet of paper once is a fantastic goal, but sometimes it's impossible. Maybe you need more information before you can delegate or dispose of a paper, or perhaps the paper raises significant questions that need to be answered before you act. If you can detour and park the paper for later follow-up, you've saved time deliberating now.

Don't park paper permanently! Create a detour file for delayed papers, but be sure you get the information you need and deal with the paper. Don't let your temporary file grow into a pile hidden in a file.

Do it

Do it is the easiest and most straightforward of all the Ds.

- ✓ Take action, either to get the task done quickly or because there's a high level of urgency associated with it:

- ✓ Tend to urgent matters. If the task moves to the top of your priorities list after you read the paper, the best course of action is to do it now. Change your priorities and work until the new priority is completed, even if it takes you the rest of the day.

- ✓ Get the task done quickly. Follow the five-minute rule: If the necessary task, phone call, response, or clarification is something only you can do, and it'll take fewer than five minutes, do it yourself right now. By the time you detour it, pick it up again later, reread it, and refocus, you'll have invested far more time than the five minutes required now.

Depot it

A depot is a place where something is deposited or stored. You can find essential tools for filing earlier in this chapter in "Streamlining Your Workspace," so you can establish an effective depot for papers you need to keep (and only the papers you need to keep).

Filing regularly

Because the task of filing is mundane, it's all too easy to allow other tasks, people, and priorities to creep into the time you set aside to deal with your piles and files, and in a few short weeks, the weeds can take over your garden again. Don't let that happen! Daily filing may not be necessary, but waiting a month or six weeks is too long. Make your time spent filing a priority. At the end of filing, your desk is devoid of piles, and you can begin filing once a week — for a much shorter time and still keep on top of your paperwork. Keep up with your filing, and you won't find it so tedious.

Schedule a weekly filing appointment with yourself and put it on your calendar. As you look ahead to assess your week and see your filing appointment, you begin mentally preparing for it. When you're prepared, you're more likely to keep your appointment with yourself, and when the time arrives, you'll be more efficient. You may find yourself throwing away more marginal items throughout the week and completing the task in less time.

When you're facing a few hours of filing, set a goal or benchmark. If you can't complete the whole project, break it down into a portion you can complete and commit to finishing that part without fail.

CHAPTER 9: TAKING TRACKABLE NOTES

In business, most people overlook the simple skill of note-taking as a time-saving tool. Most people think anyone with a pen and paper can take notes: After all, everyone learned how in junior high, right? And if you're like most people, you probably take notes on whatever's handy: sticky notes, slips of paper, cocktail napkins, envelopes, or even important documents. Wrong approach!

You can face significant time-loss and embarrassment when you later find out you lost the slip of paper where you took notes.

Whether you're using specially designed and cut pads printed with "from the desk of," a full 8 1/2-x-11-inch pad that's a color other than the standard white or yellow, or a smaller white or yellow notepad, as you need to use something that stands out.

If you know you'll need to file the notes, make sure you go with large paper so you can find it later. When you finish writing, add action items to your priority list for the following day and then drop the notes into the appropriate file for record-keeping. If your action items make it to the A level during the next day's priority sort, all you have to do is pull out the file folder and find your notes there as you left them, safe and sound. You forget to buy ice cream and pickles for your pregnant wife? That's why they're one of the worst places to jot down information. Here's why:

1. They're too small for extensive notes. You run out of room and have to transfer information to a larger note pad or, worse, to a second (and possibly third) sticky note. Then you have a sticky note stuck to

a sticky note stuck to a sticky note, and if you lose one, you lose them all.

2. Sticky notes tend to sprout legs, sticking where you don't want them to: to the wrong document headed to the wrong file. Then you're on a frantic mission to find your all-important sticky notes (and when they've hitched a ride on an unknown document going who-knows-where, your chances of finding them are slim to none).

3. Aged sticky notes lose their stick over time. More than once, I've lost important information because my sticky note came unstuck and fluttered into oblivion.

If you're not sharing a document with others, consider taking notes directly on the document rather than on a sticky note. You can take notes in the margins around the key issues in the document or use the white space at the beginning or end for summaries or more-general points.

Maintaining A Productive Environment In the Home Office

With gas prices skyrocketing and technology booming, the number of people working from home continues to grow. You can cash in on big savings in both time and money if you work from home. Here's how:

You can redirect the daily time you used to spend commuting into work, exercise, and family.

Flexible hours give you almost total control over your work schedule. If you need to get up early or stay up until midnight to meet a deadline, it's doable, and you're minutes from bed.

You spend less on lunches, dinners, and snacks, not to mention what you save on departmental gifts for holidays, parties, and other special occasions.

You chalk up lower costs for clothing. Transportation expenses such as gas, car maintenance, tolls, parking, and train or bus fare drop.

On the other hand, beware of perceptions and misperceptions that can cause your productivity at home to fizzle. In this section, I explain how to set up your office away from the office.

Creating an environment that fosters solid focus

When choosing a location for your home office, you want a place that affects your productivity and your ability to manage your time in a positive way. When the space is less than ideal, or when you struggle to focus on work even when your location is ideal, consider trying these tips to nurture your productivity:

Choose an out-of-the-way locale. Look for an area that's yours alone, removed from general traffic and noise, where you can shut the door and hang a do- not-disturb sign on the knob. The more out of the way your office is, the better use you'll make of your time.

Setting up your home office in Hub Central — the family center of your home without physical boundaries is unwise. Today's typical den off the entry doesn't provide enough physical distance. It is right in the middle of the home, so noise from both ends of the house reaches you clearly. Your family walks by numerous times, and in newer homes, the office doors are often glass, thus providing no visual barrier whatsoever.

Employ other physical barriers if your office location isn't ideal. If your home office isn't off in a private area of the house and your doors are glass, your best defense is a shade or visual barrier. When children see you "not working" (that is, thinking), they may figure it is playtime. The other necessary item is a lock on the door, which announces you're busy and uninterruptible.

Use white noise to block out other household noises. You can establish auditory boundaries by blocking household noises with white noise. White noise is a constant low-level background sound, such as static or a whirring fan, which quickly becomes inaudible but drowns out other, more disruptive noises.

Drown out distracting noise with music. The best background music for me is Baroque piano. It's simple because it's only one instrument; also, studies have shown that Baroque music stimulates the creative side of the brain. I advise against the radio because of the constantly changing style and tempo of songs, the newscasts, and disk-jockey monologues (though some people claim to work better).

Establishing boundaries and getting yourself in the work mindset

I can't emphasize enough how crafting and adhering to a set of rules for you as well as your entire family and friends increases your chance of success when you're working at home. By drawing lines between your work time and your personal time, you allow yourself to be fully present with each — and presence is a key component of productivity. To establish a solid set of boundaries for yourself, follow these suggestions:

Treat a day at the home as you would a day in your office. Start your day the same time you'd begin your commute to home-away-from-home and end it at the same you'd end your work day. Take only a half-hour lunch (but be sure to take that half-hour lunch). Regular start and stop times and set lunch breaks allow everyone to recognize your schedule and abide by it.

Start early. If you work at home, you may find, as most office workers have, that you're most productive before others arrive. In the home office world, that's before your household wakes up for the day.

Dress for success. Because you don't have to shower, shave, and don office clothes, you lose the empowering feeling you get that makes work seem like work. If you need formal dress to perform better and are negatively affected by staying in sweats or pajamas most of the day, by all means, get up, shower, and get dressed, just as you would if you were heading to the office. If you feel successful, you'll be successful, regardless of where you work.

Set goals for yourself. Set goals in terms of work completed and reward yourself for achieving them, just as you would at the office.

Don't answer personal calls during your workday. Using a home office to increase your productivity is an act of discipline. Others sometimes adopt the attitude you're not really working; people who wouldn't imagine interrupting you at the office call to chew the fat, simply because you're home. Parents are often guilty of this. Be polite but firm:

"Mom, I'm sorry. I'd love to talk, but I'm working right now. I'll call you back at five, as soon as I'm finished, okay?"

Control interruptions from your family members. Patiently train your family on your work schedule and etiquette. You may want to establish set times when you allow for interruptions.

End on time. Being available to work extended hours can diminish the quality and quantity of family time. Set boundaries. When the office door closes, let voice mail pick up work calls. Leave the office behind.

Allow yourself uninterrupted time each day to compress. A commute allows you time to shift gears. On your way home, you move from CEO, salesperson, manager, assistant, or customer service representative to Daddy, Mommy, husband, wife, partner, or Fido's master. When you exit the door of your home office, the shift is over, and you're on! So when you're done for the day, take ten minutes to decompress before you walk out the door. You may even play some relaxing music so you can leave the troubles of the day behind.

Recording your time

People often have a distorted view of how long things take. So the best way to get a clear picture of how you currently manage your time is to start making a note of exactly what you do, when, and for how long. them to cover the whole of your day. What time do you get up, how long does it take you to get ready in the morning, how long does it take you to get into work, how much time do you spend exercising, how long do you spend with friends and family, and so on? Write everything down and you'll have a better idea of where you're spending your time.

Table 2-1 shows a simple daily time log you can copy and adapt your needs. Remember, there are no right or wrong answers. At this stage you're just seeing where your time currently goes. Add as much detail as you need.

Time	Task
7.00	Get up/shower/ breakfast
8.00	Leave for work
8.30	Arrive – check emails
9.00	Team meeting
10.00	Coffee break
10.10	Write report
11.30	Emails
12.30	Lunch
13.15	Phone call
13.50	Grab paperwork and leave for meeting

14.00	Project meeting
15.10	Email follow-ups
15.30	Project work
16.00	Phone calls
16.20	Project work
17.00	Emails
17.30	Leave work
19.30	Cinema and meal with friends
11.30	Bed

At the end of the week, look at all your daily time logs and add up how much time you've spent on different types of tasks and activities such as:

✓ Breaks

✓ Emails

✓ Exercise

✓ Meetings

✓ Phone calls

✓ Socialising

✓ Writing

Now you've got a better idea of where you're spending your time each day. You can probably already see in a few obvious areas that you're not using your time very effectively; for example, times when you're interrupted or distracted, jumping from one type of task to the next.

Perhaps you've noticed the things you don't have time for like exercise, socialising, and family.

✓ Breaking down your average day

✓ What matters in time management is how much of the

✓ 24 hours in any given day you devote to each different task.

✓   Breaking your day down into time segments can help you realize just how you're spending your time at present.

Take an average work day, and estimate how many hours you spend on:

✓   Chores (shopping, cleaning, and so on)

✓   Personal activities (eating, washing, dressing, for example)

✓   Sleep

✓   Travel

✓   Work

After you add up the hours you spend on these various things, you know how much time you have left on average for yourself to exercise, to socialize, and to relax.

CHAPTER 10: USING TOOLS TO MANAGE YOUR TIME

Planning and organizing your time doesn't need to be hard work. Use the following handy tools – in combination or alone – to improve your time management.

Keeping a diary (just one, mind)

Most people have a diary, either paper-based or on their computer, perhaps even two – one for business, one for personal use. Some people have even more – one at work, one at home, and a personal one – but quite a few people don't have any system at all, keeping it all in their head or relying on other people.

How do you pick the right diary? If you choose paper-based, it doesn't matter if it's a page-a-day, or a week-at- view, as long as your diary is big enough and has enough space to write down everything you need to schedule in during your day. If you work on an hour-by-hour basis with several clients and customers you may need a page-a-day diary with space for notes. If you only attend a few meetings during the week, a week- at-a-view or two-days-to-a-page may be enough.

An A5 diary is ideal and easier to carry around in a briefcase or handbag but decide what size you need based on how you're going to use it. Electronic diaries are only useful when you're working on your computer and unless you print them out or synchronize them with a hand-held device, they're not very portable.

Seeing the big picture on a wall planner

As well as having a daily diary, having a planner pinned up on the wall is often useful. You can use a monthly calendar, or a large year planner that provides you with a big picture view of the whole year at a glance and also lets other people around you know what's happening or where you are.

In the office, a team may have one planner to track holidays, training, and out-of-office days. If you all use the same one, you know who's doing what, when and can avoid conflicts, particularly with holidays. If everyone uses the wall planner, you can colour code who's who.

Software sharing applications often enable teams to share their diaries electronically, so you can check who's where. However, having a wall planner pinned up in the office is quicker and easier to check.

At home you can have a large month or year planner for all the family to use – tracking holidays, important school days, family birthdays, social events, work commitments, and doctors' or dentist appointments.

Keeping it together with a personal organiser

Whether electronic or paper-based, personal organisers expand the function of a basic diary and can make life easier by allowing you to put all your essential information in one place. You don't have to carry around a diary, address book, and your action list separately.

Paper-based personal organisers, like Filofax and Franklin Organisers, come in all shapes and sizes. You can have page-a-day, or week-at-a-view, and there's usu- ally space to jot down appointments, lists, and notes.

Other features may include fold-out year planners, birth- day planners, expense lists, and to-do lists. Find a size and format that suits the way you work and how you're going to use it.

 Electronic personal organisers (also known as Personal Digital Assistants, or PDAs) such as the Palm Pilot, iPAQ, and even some models of mobile phones, fit easily into a pocket. Most PDAs also have the added functionality of being able to plug in to your computer and automatically synchronise with your computer system's diary and contacts (see the sidebar 'Getting in sync').

Automatic synchronization saves you having to manually re-type any updates. Skip to Chapter 18 for more details on these useful gadgets.

Logging on to computer-based tools

Most computers come with an electronic calendaring system that provides a diary and address book facility.

Microsoft Outlook is one of the most popular for Windows-based machines but others are available, some of which link in with your email system and atomatically update your email contacts, and you can schedule appointments via email.

Outlook provides a calendar, address book, task list, and email system all in one application. You can change the layout to suit the way you work, schedule in reminders, and book in appointments.

Online calendaring tools are also available, usually with your web-based email system that synchronises with your computer or hand-held device, enabling you to access your calendar when you're not at your desk. If you want, you can share your calendar across the web, choosing which events you share and who has access to them.

Plaxo, an online address book, is a convenient and time-saving way to keep up-to-date and manage and backup your contact system online. Plaxo automatically keeps you updated if your friends' and colleagues' details change. You choose what information you share and who sees it and you can have different access for personal and business contacts. Plaxo includes a calendar (which automatically updates from Outlook).

Organizing Your Time and Your Tasks

In this chapter I show you ways to structure and organise your time in the most effective way so that you get focused but also remain flexible. If you can't do everything, you need to know how to identify your most important tasks and what needs to be done first.

In this chapter you discover how to tackle those never-ending to-do lists and create something that's more realistic, productive, and actually works.

Structuring Your Time

Successful time management isn't rocket science; it goes hand in hand with effectively organizing your time. The following sections help you think about the best ways to plan and spend your time.

Creating blocks of time

Divide your day into blocks of time. Not only does doing this make it easier to plan and organise your day in advance, you also make better use of your time. Focusing on one task at a time is much more efficient than switching from one task to another as things pop into your head.

Setting aside communication time

Create blocks of time in which you handle communications – emails and outgoing phone calls. Don't fall into the trap of tackling emails and calls in dribs and drabs, otherwise you get sucked into spending longer than you intended. Set aside designated time, lay down a time limit, and stick to it.

Blocking out focused time

Some jobs, such as writing a report or proofreading a newsletter, require your complete concentration. To ensure that you can give the task the attention it requires, block out time in your diary.

If you just leave doing a task to when you feel like it, you find other things take priority. But if you've already scheduled in the time for the task, there's less reason to put it off or be interrupted by other work coming in. Your time is already committed.

If you need some quiet, creative time, go some- where different, away from the distractions of your normal workspace. For example, getting up early and working from home for a couple of hours enables you to get more done away from the distractions of the office.

Factoring in circumstances

Unless you're clairvoyant, you can't plan for every eventuality. For example:

Your boss turns up and asks you to do an urgent piece of work by the end of the day.

You come up against a problem and it takes time to fix it. For example, your computer crashes just at the critical moment and you lose everything you've been working on. You have to wait a day or so for the repair, or you have to rely on your backups.

A report you're writing needs a vital piece of information and you can't get hold of the person who can provide it because he or she is away on holiday until next week.

You get a call reminding you about a piece of work you'd forgotten about and you need to get it done now.

You underestimate how long a task takes.

In addition, bear the following in mind when blocking out time in your diary:

When you book a meeting in your diary, the time involved isn't just about the meeting itself. You may have preparation work to do, travel time, and after the meeting, follow-up and minutes or a report to produce. Block out time for both pre- and post- meeting work as well as the event itself.

Be aware of the energy requirements of different days (see the following section 'Working with your natural tendencies'). If you've had an intense day of meetings, book in some time for admin work or for catching up. Training courses and workshops can be mentally and physically demanding – whether you're the one giving them or participating.

When you get back from holiday, set aside at least the first half-day for dealing with your emails and paperwork, otherwise you fall straight back into work mode and never catch up. Try not to book up a heavy day of meetings for your first day back, so you have time to catch up or check in with your staff or colleagues.

Working with your natural tendencies

When planning your time, work to your strengths and create a structure that best fits your natural tendencies.

Know when your most productive time of day is and when you prefer doing certain types of tasks and plan around those times:

Early bird: Some people work best first thing in the morning, which can be a good time for creativity. If you find you're more efficient and productive in the morning, use the morning to do tasks that require you to be at your best or need your concentration. Don't set aside time to work on a complex report or something that requires your concentration in the afternoon when you're more likely to hit the post-lunch slump, or in the evening when you're tired.

Night owl: Some people get steadily more alert and effective as the day goes on. Perhaps you struggle to get going in the morning and feel as if you're just ticking over, but are turbo-charged after lunch and into the evening. You may find you focus best late at night, when it's quiet. If this is you, plan your day around your tendencies. Don't try getting up at 6 a.m. to write a report if you know you can do it better and quicker at 2 p.m.

Also think about how the week pans out for you. Certain days of the week may make better sense when scheduling in particular tasks. For example, you may hit the ground running on a Monday morning but be ready to go home by Thursday. Alternatively, you may find you have a peak of activity on a Friday when you're keen to clear things out at the end of the week and go home with a clean slate.

Doing varied tasks, little and often

Your mind can easily become bored if you spend too long on a particular task. So don't plan to sit down for hours on end focusing on just one task in a long, intense session. Break a task down into small bites and work through little and often.

The longer you spend doing one thing, the more inef- fective you actually become. You're more efficient and productive when you do short bursts of activity:

✓ You won't get so distracted if you know you've only got a limited amount of time on which to work on a task.

✓ Time out during a task refreshes you. Your mind has a chance to process things and you can come up with new thoughts and solutions, particularly if you have a difficult problem to deal with or a mental block. Having a time limit – such as 10, 20, or 30 minutes – can increase the rate at which you work, so you actually get more done.

✓ Working on a difficult or odious task for just a short period of time doesn't seem as bad as having to do it all in one go!

And while you're blocking out short amounts of time for tasks, you can also introduce a bit of variety to spice up your day. Injecting a bit of variety into your everyday work helps you keep interested, energetic, and motivated.

Consider the following ideas:

✓ Mix high-energy or intense tasks with something less demanding. Work hard, and then sit back a bit.

✓   Spread out your energy.

✓   Switch from a task that requires you to be analytical to one that requires you to work more creatively. Think about engaging the left and right sides of your brain as you work. You'll find you're able to focus better.

✓   Can you do the same thing in a different location? Working from home or working at a different office from time to time can add variety to your working environment, keeping your mind stimulated.

Scheduling in 'me time'

Spending all day sitting at your desk, hunched over your computer keyboard, or with the phone attached to your head, leaves you tired, both physically and mentally. Include breaks in the structure of your day:

1. Do some stretches

2. Step away from your desk and walk around the office, or even better, get outside for some freshair.

3. Grab a healthy snack or a drink of water.

4. Take some quiet time and just relax.

5. Building 'me time' into your day is just as important as fitting in the million and one jobs you have to do.

Organizing Your Tasks

The following sections have one key, unifying theme lists. Forget relying on your memory to tell you everything you need to do, or working amid piles of scribbled to-do lists – in the following sections, I show you how using simple lists helps you to manage your workload effectively.

Binning to-do lists

If you're like most people, you have a to-do list. Your list likely consists of an A4 sheet of paper (or several) or perhaps a document on your computer. You continually add tasks to the list and occasionally cross things off.

Actually I don't like using to-do lists and I suspect others don't either. Such lists can be a bit of a double-edged sword. Although they're a useful tool when used correctly – and they create structure in a busy day – the items on the list have a tendency to be things you want to do and not things that actually get done.

Your to-do list then becomes a source of frustration and stress. You constantly add tasks, and end up demoralised and overwhelmed as the list grows longer and longer and you never seem to get to the end of it.

My advice? Ditch the to-do list, and instead, use action lists (see the following sections). An action list comprises tasks you're going to action rather an endless list of jobs that you'd get round to . . . if only you had the time.

Prioritising your tasks

It's rarely possible to get everything done you'd like to, so you have to make choices about what you need to work on. When you have a limited amount of time available you make a choice about what to work on immediately and what to leave until later – you prioritize your tasks.

You may choose to reorganise your filing system be- cause it'll make finding things easier and you'll have a great sense of satisfaction when it's done. However, if you've chosen to do this instead of doing the report that your boss needs by the end of the day, you need to rethink your priorities.

Prioritising your tasks is essential. However many tasks you have on your list, you can establish a logical order in which they need to be done.

CHAPTER 11: EFFECTIVE USE OF THE TO-DO LIST

There's nothing new about the to-do list. Folks have been jotting down lists of things they need to do and then checking each item off the list as they do them for a very long time. The more you need to do, and the more pressure you feel to do it, the more helpful the list can be.

When you try to get more done in the same amount of time, you run the risk of overload, a phenomenon known in computer lingo as "thrashing," when the computer gets too many commands at once and gets stuck trying to decide what to do first.

There are other dangers inherent in developing a list of tasks the night before or during the morning of each workday. To illustrate those dangers, let's look at a sample to-do list, one that makes just about every possible mistake. Here, then, is:

The To-Do List From Hell

We'll impose a mid-level of organization, less than a minute-by-minute script but more than a simple list of tasks.

To do before work

1. Exercise: 100 situps, 50 pushups, 25 squats

2. Review agenda and materials for staff meeting

3. Read The Wall Street Journal

Morning commute (17 minutes)

Listen to motivational self-help CD on time management

Morning

1. Answer faxes, overnight mail, voice mail, e-mail (8 a.m.–9 a.m.)

2. Staff meeting (9 a.m.–10:30 a.m.)

3. Organize research for quarterly report (10:30 a.m.–11:45 a.m.)

4. Drive to lunch meeting (15 minutes)

5. Lunch meeting (noon-1:30 p.m.)

Afternoon

1. Write draft of quarterly report (1:45 p.m.–3:00 p.m.)

2. Meet with committee on workplace expectations (3 p.m.–4:30 p.m.)

3. Afternoon commute (18 minutes — pick up dry-cleaning)

That's it. There's your workday, all laid out. Do all that and you'll likely be laid out, too.

Notice that your ability to accomplish all the tasks on your list depends on split-second timing. Everything must go perfectly — no traffic jams, no emergencies, no interruptions.

When's the last time you had a perfect day — no traffic jams, no emergencies, and no interruptions? That's what I thought.

The Day As You Really Live It

You sleep through the snooze alarm twice. (You're exhausted from your wrestling match with yesterday's to-do list.) No time for exercise or, for that matter, breakfast — which didn't even make it onto the original list. You're down two, feeling guilty and grouchy before you've even gotten started.

You glance at your meeting notes, skim the left-hand column on the front page of the Journal, and sprint to the car. You're in luck. The car starts, even though you've put off getting it serviced — no time. No idiot ruins your day by getting into an accident ahead of you, and traffic flows fairly smoothly.

Even so, the commute takes 18.5 minutes, so you're already running ninety seconds behind. You didn't get to listen to your motivational CD, either, because the CD player in the car jammed. (Better put "get CD player fixed" on your future to-do list.)

You can anticipate the rest. (You don't have to anticipate it. You've lived it.) You don't even get close to going through all the voice mail, let alone the e-mail.

The meeting starts late and runs long — don't they always? It's too late to tackle the quarterly report, and you spend the rest of the morning answering the phone and battling e-mail.

After a lunch you didn't taste and a meeting you didn't need, you finally get a few minutes for those notes for the quarterly report. You're tired, grouchy, full of a chicken enchilada that refuses to settle down and let itself be digested, and preoccupied with the meeting you've got to get to in a few minutes. No wonder the report refuses to organize itself.

Another meeting (starts late, runs long), another snarling, gut-wrenching commute, a wasted stop at the dry-cleaners (in your rush this morning, you left your claim ticket on the bureau).

Another day shot

And now it's time to start the second shift, the workday put in at home sweet home.

Pretty dismal scene, isn't it? And not really that much of an exaggeration.

Did the to-do list help? Sure. It provided a record of what you didn't get done while you were doing other things, and it helped you to go to bed guilty and frustrated by every unchecked item.

What went wrong? You failed to plan for the unplanned. You weren't realistic about your own capacities or about the real time required to do things. You left important stuff off the list that needed to be done, and spent too much time on low value busywork.

In short, this wasn't a to-do list. It was a wish list, a fantasy, an unattainable dream, an invitation to frustration and fatigue.

Suggestions For Creating A Healthy To-Do List

The following list of suggestions incorporates some effective techniques for creating an effective to-do list. If some of the suggestions seem to contradict others, it's because they do. It is hoped that some techniques will appeal to certain readers. Embrace those that work for you.

Don't Put Too Much on It

This is fundamental. Master this one, and everything else falls into place.

Be realistic in your expectations and your time estimates. Make a real-world list, not an itinerary for fantasyland. Otherwise, you'll spend the day running late, running scared, and just flat-out running to catch up. You won't even have time to notice how your efficiency drops as you become cranky and exhausted.

Think about what absolutely needs your attention, tasks that no one else can do, and put those things on your list. Because you've planned your big projects, calculated how much time they require, and when each stage needs to be completed (haven't you?), put the must-do steps on your list.

But don't jam the list. By putting the absolutely most important, must-do items on your list, you'll find that there is no room for the less important, optional, and even forgettable tasks. That's okay. Let the list help you organize, keep on task, and get the important jobs done.

If by some miracle things take less time than you had allowed for, rejoice! You've given yourself the gift of found time, yours to spend however you want and need to.

Put Some Air in It

Overestimate the commute time. Figure in the wait before the meeting, the time spent on hold, the traffic backup. Due to Murphy's Law, planning for a possible traffic jam ensures that it won't occur, and you will arrive early at your destination. Allowing yourself just enough time for your trip, however, guarantees a delay. Now you know.

List Possibilities, Not Imperatives

This speaks more to your frame of mind when you make the list than to the specific notations on that list. You're listing those tasks that you hope, want, and, yes, need to finish during the day. You're not creating a blueprint for the rest of the universe, and your plans don't have the force of natural law.

What happens if you don't get to everything on your list?

What happens if you wake up simply too ill to crawl out of bed, let alone tackle the crammed workday?

I'm talking serious sick here, not the borderline sore throat and headache that might keep you in bed on a Saturday, but not on a workday. In a way, the serious sickness is easier, because you don't have to decide whether or not to attempt to go to work, and you don't have to feel guilty about staying in bed while the rest of the world is tending to business. (Depending on your tolerance for pain and your level of guilt, you might have to be near death to achieve this state.)

Let's suppose you're sick enough to have to stay flat on your back in bed for two days, and you can barely wobble around the house in bathrobe and slippers on the third. In all, you miss an entire week of work.

Meanwhile, what happened to the stuff on your to-do list?

The meetings went on without you. Folks figured out they could live without the quarterly report for another week. You've got 138 messages on voice mail (sixty-two of them from the same person), 178 e-mails (fifty-two of them copies of replies and replies to replies by multiple recipients on a single question), and a desk awash in memos, faxes, mail, and other unnatural disasters. You take stuff home for a week, trying to get caught up.

 That's bad, but it isn't that bad. You didn't die. You didn't lose a loved one. Western civilization did not grind to a halt. Commerce and government managed to struggle on without you.

It's too late to respond to some of those urgent e-mails and messages, but it turns out they really didn't need a response after all.

Try to remember that the next time you're relatively healthy, but nevertheless falling behind on the day's tasks.

None of this is to suggest that what you do isn't important — at least as important as playing baseball.

You need to keep things in proper perspective.

Schedule Your Tasks

If you can assign a time slot in your day to accomplish a particular task, there is a much greater likelihood you will actually do it. You will be mentally prepared, committed to tackling the job, and less prone to distractions if it's scheduled with a beginning and end point. With onerous tasks in particular, scheduling a one-hour or just a half-hour period makes the job less threatening.

Don't Carve the List in Stone

Your list has to be flexible if it's going to do you any good. You have to be able to change it, digress from it, flip it on its ear, add to it, wad it up and toss it in the recycle bin — if it's really going to help.

 Find a flexible format that works for you. If you like an intricate grid system, with squares for every five minutes during the day, go for the grid. If you keep your list on a PDA, complete with abbreviations that only you understand, that's fine. If crayon on butcher paper is more your style, start scrawling.

Don't try to fit a format; none are perfect. Try some or all of them until you find or create a format that works for you.

Order Creatively

Make sure the most important tasks get done before you drown in a sea of relative trivia. Answer the e-mail first if it's absolutely the top priority on your list. If it isn't, schedule it for later in the day, or if possible, establish one or two periods at the same time every day to tackle e-mail.

Don't do it first simply because it's there, demanding attention, or because it's relatively easy, or because you've gotten into the habit of doing it first. It's too easy to be caught up in an extensive e-mail conversation on a marginal project, and find that half of your morning is shot.

Try to vary your pace, alternating difficult and easy, long and short, jobs requiring creative thought with rote functions. Change activities often enough to keep fresh.

Attack mentally taxing jobs when you're most alert and energetic. For most of us, this means first thing in the morning. If you save them for later, you're admitting you aren't going to work on them.

Turn the Big Jobs into Small Jobs

When large tasks are involved, it's important to define and isolate (divide and conquer) the components of the task. In fact, it's essential to break down a large task into small tasks to understand what steps are involved and in what order they must be completed in order to finish the larger goal.

If one of your tasks is writing a product development plan, for example, and you know the amount of time and effort it will consume, defining the parts of the plan will make it much more controllable. You may avoid the task if it's "write a product development plan," but "collect competitive data" is much more approachable. By allotting just half an hour to this step, you're more likely to do it and reap that sense of accomplishment towards the overall goal.

Schedule Breaks, Time-Out Time, and Little Rewards

Most of us schedule "rest" for last — if we schedule it at all. By the time we get to it, if we get to it, it's too late to do us any good.

If you don't put rest on the list, you won't do it. So put it on the list with a start point and an end point. And don't save it for last. Plan the rest for when it will do you some good, before you become too tense or exhausted. Brief rests at the right times will help you maintain a steady, efficient work pace.

Instead of waiting until the end of the day for that 15 minutes of pleasure reading, for example, schedule three five-minute reading breaks during the day. You may even want and need to schedule that game of catch with your kid or that walk around the neighborhood with your spouse. You can even use software that will alert you to your scheduled breaks so you don't have to remember them.

Schedule Long-Range Personal Goals

You know you should do some serious financial planning. You know you should have a current will. You know you should create a systematic plan for home maintenance and repair.

If you know all that and never seem to get to it — put it on the schedule. And, again, if you schedule these goals in manageable steps, you'll be much more likely to actually do them.

Be Ready to Abandon the List

"If you only write the story that is planned," writer and teacher Ellen Hunnicutt tells her students, "you miss the story that is revealed."

The same goes for the story of your life. The most important thing you do all day, all year, or even all lifetime, may never appear on any to-do list or show up on the day planner. Never get so well organized and so scheduled that you stop being alert to life's possibilities, the chance encounter, the sudden inspiration.

Ways To Get A Fast Start

Prepare Mentally

Back at the turn of the century, a man named Charles Haanel called the subconscious mind "a benevolent stranger, working on your behalf." For all our subsequent research on the working of the brain, that remains a perceptive description.

You can get that subconscious stranger working for you on any job you have to perform.

The night before the job, settle in your mind exactly what you want to accomplish the following day. You're not issuing orders here. You're not telling the subconscious how you intend to do the job. That's part of the conscious planning stage.

You're simply planting the idea, giving that larger mind that exists outside of conscious thought time to mull and sift, combining images and ideas, amassing energy and positive attitude.

Instead of letting the subconscious disaster tapes play, visualize yourself performing exactly as you wish. This is particularly helpful if you're going to speak to a group or otherwise put yourself before an audience.

This isn't a matter of "wishing will make it so." Positive visualization won't cast a magic spell over your audiences. But it will affect your behavior, helping you call forth your best effort by concentrating energies and consciousness. This preparation will give your mind an opportunity to rehearse an event before the fact, and to call forth "memories" when it actually takes place, rather than react with surprise.

Prepare Physically

An obvious step is to have your physical tools assembled and accessible before you begin the job. If possible, stake out a specific place for the work, where you can keep everything you need within easy reach and not have to stow it between work sessions. That way, you eliminate time spent pitching camp and then tearing it down again each time.

Also, when you become accustomed to doing a job in a specific place, you'll be focused and ready to work as soon as you enter that place. This is another example of mind conditioning; you're training your mind to perform a certain function in a certain place. This place doesn't have to be fancy or even private. It just has to be yours, and it has to have the tools you need.

Map the Terrain

Before you begin the trip, figure out exactly where you want to go, and what the destination looks like. This is another basic requirement in order to reach a successful conclusion, but it's astonishing how often the trigger will be pulled before the gun is properly aimed. Remind yourself of your purpose. What's in it for you?

For your organization? For the client or customer? If you can't answer these questions, save yourself time and effort — and ensure that you'll do a better job — by taking a few moments now to get the information you need and to focus on what you hope to accomplish. If you still aren't sure, seek out the authorization, approval, or verification you need. Again, a few minutes spent here can save hours later. And you'll work more efficiently and confidently.

If the work involves several stages, write them down first. Don't try to create the sort of orderly outline only an English teacher could love. Just jot down the steps or ideas in the order they occur to you. Then number the items in proper sequence. If it is still difficult to create this simple list of steps, by now you should be alerted to the fact that you have a problem.

Start Anywhere

If you aren't ready to start at the beginning, start someplace else.

You can't escape certain sequences. A plumber has to turn off the water before disassembling the pipes, for example. But jobs often contain a great deal of flexibility.

The finished product may need to be assembled in the proper order, but you don't necessarily have to tackle the components in that order.

A director shoots a movie in the most practical sequence, getting all the location shots before returning to the studio for the interiors, for example.

These separate scenes become the raw material for the finished movie. If the director and the editors do their jobs well, the viewer can't tell (and doesn't care) in what order the scenes were shot; the movie tells a coherent, entertaining story.

The seams don't show. When you're thinking your way through a problem, it doesn't matter where you start. Often, it is more productive to start at the end of the puzzle and work backwards. Just start somewhere.

Lock Out the Critics

We all make mistakes. Some of us get to make ours in private, and we can give ourselves the chance to fix them before anybody else sees them. But when a quarterback throws an interception, every football fan in the stadium sees him do it (and more will see the replay or read about it), and there's no way he can pull the ball back and take the play over. Lots of us work that way also. There's no time for a redo, there's barely enough time to get it done the first time, and we feel the eyes of the boss or customers on us as we work our way through a challenge.

It's a two-step process, first the doing, and then the judgment. Just as an NFL quarterback has to shut out the howling of the mob and concentrate on the receiver, you have to shut out concerns about judgment during the process of creation. If you don't, you won't take a chance, try out an idea, risk a "failure" in the eyes of the invisible judge.

Stop Before You Need To

Momentum is a wonderful feeling, especially when we've got a lot to do and not much time to do it. An interruption is the last thing you want when the job is going well. Common sense tells you to keep working until you're finished. If you can't finish the job in one sitting, you work until you're exhausted or until you run into a snag you can't work your way through. But it can make a lot more sense to stop before you get too tired and before you reach a snag.

If you stop because you're stuck, you carry that "stuckness" with you until the next work session. You'll sit back down to the task and immediately be faced with the same problem that stopped you previously. And if you give yourself too much time between work sessions, you'll build up an aversion to the task, the very material blocks are made of.

But if you've stopped in midstride, sure of the next step you'll take, you'll come back to the job confident and even eager. You won't have to waste any time getting back into the groove, because you won't have gotten out of it. This is a technique used by many successful writers, who would have a significant problem starting up if they hadn't stopped while "on a roll."

There is an exception to this "rule" and whether the rule or its exception applies to you depends on the type of person you are, and how you tend to work through problems. Most of us just keep punching until we make a hole in the wall, but some individuals receive problem-solving inspiration while engaged in activities not directly related to the task.

I knew one fellow who did his best thinking while running; he'd break from a task when he hit a snag, go for a run, and by the time he returned he typically had found a solution. If your mind works in thisnontraditional way — like setting a PC to defrag while you go off and do something else — then don't tamper with your system. Encourage it and use it to your advantage.

CHAPTER 12: THE COMEBACK KID

T ime is running out and your team is trailing. Things look bleak; your guys have no chance; there's not enough time left. But the team, made of sterner stuff, reaches down deep, and with an effort suitable for a Hollywood epic, rallies in the final seconds to win. The fans go wild, drowning out the commentator who's screaming hysterically, "I can't believe it! I can't believe it!"

You know you're running your rally When …

✓ You charge from meeting to meeting, appointment to appointment, with no time to gather your thoughts;

✓ You've taken lunch at your desk so often, your keyboard's clogged with crumbs;

✓ The ringing phone makes you jump;

✓ You feel one bad surprise away from throwing up your hands and screaming;

✓ A longtime friend calls to tell you she's coming to town and would love to see you, but you make excuses because there's just no way you can spare the time;

✓ You aren't getting any exercise, but you feel exhausted;

✓ You crawl into bed at last — and can't fall asleep.

We all go through days, even weeks like that. For short spells, it can even be exhilarating — as long as we can keep one jump ahead of disaster. But the longer you sustain this killer pace, the more you suffer and the less efficient you become not just in your work, but in every aspect of life.

Call A Time Out

If you wait for life to ease up and for the bad surprises to stop coming, you may wait too long. You have to call an end to the rally and start working at a more normal pace, for yourself, your loved ones, and your colleagues. But the more you worry about relaxing, the more tense you become. What now?

You need to learn how to slow down the pace, to normalize your efforts so they're consistent and effective rather than enduring a daily train wreck. By relaxing mind and body four or five times a day, you can achieve the control you need to reduce stress and be more productive.

Taking Mini-Vacations Every Day

Take your break before you need it. Don't wait to be exhausted, and don't wait to be stuck. Break your momentum — and the buildup of stress and fatigue with a sanity break in the midst of the chaos. Make the break a good habit, three or four times a day.

<u>Ways To Go On Vacation Without Leaving Your Desk</u>

The Breath Break

Here's the simplest, cheapest vacation you'll ever take. For two minutes, just breathe. Take air way down into your belly. You should actually be able to feel your stomach rise with the intake of breath.

But haven't you been breathing already? Sort of. But as you hurry, and as you feel the pressure build inside you, your breath becomes shallow, and you don't get the

oxygen you need. You'll especially notice this when you have to speak in front of a group. Your voice rises and gets squeaky, and your throat becomes dry and sore.

To combat the ill effects of this oxygen debt, you don't have to empty your mind or chant a mantra or wrap yourself into a yoga position. All you have to do is breathe deeply and slowly for a couple of minutes three, four, even five times a day. In private, with your feet up and your eyes closed would be nice, of course, but you can take a breath break in the middle of a meeting, behind the wheel of the car, or on the phone. Nobody needs to know you're sneaking oxygen.

The Continental Drift

Think of a place of perfect contentment in your life, or hearken back to a time when you were truly relaxed and at peace. (You may have to go all the way back to summer vacation during your elementary school years.)

Or create an imaginary oasis.

Then go there for two minutes.

Shut out everything else, close your eyes, and create the scene in your mind. See, hear, feel it. Let warmth and peace wash over you.

You may feel goofy the first few times you try this, but once you've mastered the technique, you'll return refreshed after just a couple of minutes, and you'll know you can go back again soon.

Pack Up Your Troubles

Something bothering you? Visualize and get rid of it.

Picture your nemesis, hot branding iron in hand, sneering at you, ready to poke and prod. If your anger and frustration has an abstract source, give it a specific shape. Lack of time making you crazy? Picture a clock gone berserk, its hands spinning out of control. Or make time into a huge Indiana Jones-style boulder, rolling toward you with desperate speed.

Then put the image into a bubble and imagine that bubble floating slowly up and away, becoming smaller and smaller until it finally disappears.

The Shoulder Shrug

We tend to take out our tensions on specific parts of our bodies. Shoulders are one of my favorite targets.

Without knowing I'm doing it, I tense my shoulders as I work. If I don't catch myself, I end up with a sore neck and shoulders and a pounding headache.

I can break the tension, save my shoulders, and avert the headache by remembering to relax my shoulders and rotate them slowly and gently for a couple of minutes. On particularly bad days, the results are dramatic. My shoulders seem to drop several inches, and a soothing warmth flows up my neck.

I never even realize how tense I am until I unclench my muscles and relax. How about you? Are you tensing and clenching while you work?

The Phrase for the Day

This one takes a bit of preparation, but it's well worth the effort. Collect pithy bits of wisdom, interesting observations, intriguing fragments of ideas, funny phrases, anything that snags your fancy. You can catch them everywhere — from the media, from conversation, from your own boundlessly creative and endlessly curious mind. Get in the habit of jotting them down as you run across them.

If you find that it's too time consuming to find these phrases on your own, purchase a calendar of daily wisdom or jokes or observations — whatever triggers you most effectively.

When it's time for a break, pull out one of the phrases, read it a couple of times, and let yourself chew on it for two minutes. Don't direct your thoughts. Just let them wander where they will.

The Object of Your Affection

Hold a picture of a person you treasure, an object that has special meaning for you, or a talisman (like that lucky silver dollar you've lugged around with you for years). Spend two minutes with it, again letting your thoughts roam.

Why The Two-Minute Break Works

Will a two-minute break really do you any good?

Yes. It really will. But you may feel uncomfortable breathing from your tummy the first few times, and you may not notice the effects right away. But if you stick with it, you'll feel the difference.

Here's why.

As you come under fire in the daily wars, your body instinctively reacts, tensing muscles and doling out emergency rations of adrenaline and other natural uppers, getting you ready to fight your enemies or run away from them. These automatic responses will work against you when you've got no one to fight and nowhere to run.

These reactions can build on themselves, and you can get caught in a dangerous loop. You sense danger, and your body responds. That response in turn seems to verify the perception of danger and triggers still more response.

No wonder you can't relax at the end of the day!

But the cycle can work for you as well as against you. If you can relax your body slowing your breathing, calming your heart — by taking a two-minute break, your panic will subside. You'll regain focus, clarity, and energy.

CHAPTER 13: LEARNING TO SAY "NO"

Are you one of those busy people who can always be counted on to take on an additional job? You'll not only serve on the volunteer board, you'll chair it, take the meeting notes, edit the newsletter, and head up the recruitment subcommittee.

✓ "I just don't know how you do it all," folks tell you.

✓ Do you? Do you know why you do? And have you considered how much that extra work is costing you?

✓ "I just don't have your energy," folks tell you, or "I can't ever seem to find the time" — right before they ask you to take on another job.

✓ "We can always count on you!" they gush when you say "yes."

Your willingness to serve speaks well for you. You help because you believe in the cause and because you want to make your family, your workplace, and your community better places. You're a helper, a problem solver, a doer. You're community-minded, a team player, in sports parlance the "go-to person."

But you may be doing more than you should — for your own physical and mental health, for the well-being of your loved ones, and for your ability to be effective and efficient. To find out, examine your motives, all of them for saying "yes" to each task.

Why We May Have Trouble Saying "No"

1. Looking for love in all the right causes. You do indeed earn the

gratitude and approval of your peers when you shoulder their burdens. The need for their approval and acceptance may in part be the reason you say "yes." Behind this desire may even lurk the fear that, if you don't work so hard, those around you will stop accepting you.

2. The guilt syndrome. "It's difficult to say 'no' when someone asks you to serve on a not-for-profit board, or chair a committee, or attend a fund-raiser for a very worthy cause," "When we decline, we are often inclined to shoulder a subsequent burden of guilt, because 'superwoman' failed to come through as expected." Sometimes that guilt can cloud our objectivity.

3. The myth of indispensability. Rather than kindness, your effort may in part be motivated by arrogance. Perhaps you don't let others do the job because, deep down, you don't believe anyone else can do it or do it as well as you can. You've taken to heart the adage "If you want a job done right, do it yourself."

4. The fear of expendability. What if you didn't show up for work and nobody noticed? On some basic, subconscious level, you may be afraid that the moment you stop all your efforts, people will discover they don't really need you at all. Or, you may feel this on a very conscious and practical level, and need to reinforce your importance to your organization.

5. The Martyr Syndrome. Do you secretly enjoy bearing the burdens of an overworked schedule? Do you believe it's your lot in life to suffer — in a time management sense?

Reasons three and four may seem mutually exclusive, but they're not. It's quite possible to feel both ways at the same time. Just as you can be in a "love/hate relationship," you can feel both indispensable and expendable.

If any of these motivations apply to you, and you're able to admit it, you may be saying "yes" because it satisfies some need or quells a fear more painful than the loss of time from accepting more duties.

Understanding this about yourself is the first big step in summoning the courage to say "no."

Why All That "Yes" Sneaks Up On You

Glaucoma is a gradual hardening of the eyeball, which if left untreated, can cause blindness. It's an especially insidious disease; because the impairment is so gradual, the victim is often able to make subtle, unconscious compensations for a slowly shrinking field of vision, becoming aware of the disease only when it's too late to treat it.

Making too many commitments can be like that, too.

"The problem with clutter in our lives, like clutter in our closets, is it arrives one piece at a time, never in basketfuls," Benson Wright notes. "It's not too difficult to refuse a huge, overwhelming load of additional responsibilities; it's tough, however, to decline 'just one more.'"

Add up all the extra tasks you perform, anything above and beyond what's required. Check your planner and look closely at time slots in the evening and on weekends, your "personal" time.

Here's the start of one person's list:

- ✓ Coach a Y basketball team
- ✓ Chair the workplace expectations committee at the office
- ✓ Coordinate United Way fundraising in the department
- ✓ Serve as recording secretary for the church council
- ✓ And on and on …

These are all good, worthwhile things to do. Somebody should do them. But does it have to be you in every instance?

The items on your list are all good, worthy endeavors, too. You probably genuinely enjoy doing them. We tend to enjoy the things we do well and gravitate toward these tasks when we have a choice. Time management would be a lot easier if there were obvious time wasters on your list and tasks you dreaded doing.

CHAPTER 14: TIME MANAGEMENT FOR STUDENTS

Full-time and part-time students face unique time management issues, as well as experiencing concerns common to most people with busy schedules. We present some tips that students can use to better manage their time.

Principles Of Time Management For Students

1. Every individual performs better at certain times of the day.

You should use these periods when you are able to concentrate more fully as study times for your hardest classes, rather than errands or relaxing. It may require experimentation to determine when your best time(s) occur unless you already know that you're a "morning person" or "night person."

2. Tackle difficult subjects before the easier or more enjoyable ones. Work on one subject at a time for maximum focus.

3. Try studying in short time blocks divided by short breaks. You'll tire less easily and your brain will continue to process information during the breaks.

4. Pick a study area and always use it exclusively for studying.

This trains your mind to accomplish what you want to with minimal "start up." The area should be comfortable (but not too comfortable), quiet, have good lighting, and low traffic or other distractions. Your bed, by the way, is for sleeping.

5. Use down time effectively. Have index cards with formulas or anything you need to memorize, so you can study them while doing laundry, between classes, or waiting in line. This works well for material that exists in discrete units and requires significant review before it's absorbed. Audio material can be reviewed while on the bus or walking to class. Always carry a book wherever you go in case of unforeseen delays in traffic, at airports, etc.

6. Don't forget to sleep and eat properly. It's easy to sacrifice your sleep, and you may not miss it until you crash. There will be times you need to pull an all-nighter, but making the effort to get a regular night's sleep on a regular basis will make you much more effective during waking hours. Your health is important; eat in balance to maintain it properly.

7. If your mind tends to wander while you're trying to study, keep a notepad with you to record your thoughts. This will clear your mind so you can refocus on your studies. If a particular problem won't go away, develop a quick, mini-plan for dealing with it complete with steps and schedule. Write it down, then go back to the books. (Like an extra book, it's a good idea to keep a notepad or notebook with you all the time to catch stray thoughts and ideas, both brilliant and mundane.)

8. Respect your study time and encourage others to respect it as well. You need to be left alone during these times even if your roommates or classmates feel like partying. This includes telephone interruptions as well. Turn off the phone if you need to. Enforcing time for study will require tact, resolve, and maturity.

9. All work and no play makes the student a dull person. The college student should carve out time to experience social life as well as the academic. All students, even part timers, can benefit from sharing thoughts and opinions with their classmates. Good time management will permit a balance of activities.

10. Plan your day. Know each morning where you need to go and what

you need to accomplish that day. Bring with you what you'll use that day, including lunch, so you don't waste time later.

11. Reward yourself when you meet your goals. The rewards can be no more than an extra five minutes of break time, but they support behaviors you're trying to adopt, and even minor bonuses will be positive and worthwhile reinforcements.

12. You've had a busy day and are exhausted looking at another busy day tomorrow. Before cashing in, do one more task, even if it's just looking at a page of notes for 30 seconds.

You'll have a greater sense of accomplishment for the day that you'll carry forward to tomorrow.

13. If you're having trouble with a particular class, with study skills, or some other problem, seek out assistance as soon as possible before the issue gets out of control. Colleges want their students to succeed and most have extensive support systems available for the asking. Don't waste your time struggling with a problem alone.

14. Class time is important, obviously. Make sure you use it effectively by being alert, prepared, ready to absorb as much as possible. You are doing yourself a disservice by attending class when you're too tired or hungover to concentrate. It's better to sleep in, borrow a classmate's notes later, and promise yourself not to miss another class.

Undoubtedly, you are already practicing some of these techniques, and have tried and discarded others. Try those that are new to you to determine if they're beneficial. They can not only help you to use your time more effectively, but will also improve your educational experience.

Project Management

Proper time management techniques are essential to good project management. In fact, project management considers time an important resource, and the timing of activities essential to achieving the project's goals. This and the fact that so many workers are responsible for projects makes it valuable to consider how time and project management are interrelated.

Those interested in improving their time management skills can benefit greatly from learning the principles of project management. And whether you are the project manager or project team member, you should take the responsibility to understand and do your best to follow these principles.

Where To Start

A project starts with a specification. This is the definition of the project and includes, at the very least, a statement of the problem that the project hopes to solve.

The wise project manager knows that the specification contains errors, ambiguities, and misdirections.

Depending on the complexity of the project, the specification will change many times before the project is completed, and probably with increasing frequency as the deadline draws closer. Everyone who was involved in the creation of the specification or who will use the specification knows this, but will embrace some of its inaccuracies to the bitter end, fighting for the errors of his choice. One part of the specification that will not change, even if it's completely arbitrary, is the due date.

The project manager must call meetings, assemble all the project stakeholders, and review the specification point by point until everyone has the same understanding (and it's in writing) of what is required, when it's required, and the cost. The time and effort spent in this initial step of project definition will save time later, and will protect careers. The project demands this effort and the project team deserves it.

A complex project may take months to complete, involve hundreds of people, dozens of suppliers, and has the potential to make or break an organization. So, spending time on getting it right the first time is understandable. But minor projects or tasks so small that they can't even be termed "projects," can and will benefit from the same initial definition step.

If you or your team is responsible for a task and you don't have a clear idea of what your goal looks like, then you are doomed. You can go through all of the rest of the steps to reach your goal, but may miss it by a mile. At this stage you should look at:

The big picture

Does this project make sense, and will the parts work when they're put together?

Teams

If the project requires a team and particularly if it requires more than one, how will team members work together, communicate, divide or share responsibilities?

Time

You have an end date, but the individual steps required have their own schedules. Are they achievable?

Costs

Budgets are great until you exceed one, then various people become agitated to various degrees. Build in a cushion, the largest one you can get away with.

Human resources

Teams can consist of consultants, hired help, freelancers, vendors, and others. They all need to play by the same game plan and be committed for the project to work.

Other resources

Any materials and equipment necessary to do the work needs to be specified. If new software is required, for example, it will need to be purchased, installed, and may require training. Check that costs have been correctly estimated and time built in so the team is not expected to be using software before it has learned how, or hardware before it's installed.

Building A Project Framework

The next step in managing a project is determining what you actually need to do and how to do it. This is done by converting the specification into a set of tasks or activities. The activities need to be simple enough that they can be managed, linked to each other logically, and ordered.

For simple projects, there may be only a few straightforward steps; for large projects, the steps may need to be broken down several times and the linking can become complex. The steps are descriptions in themselves, with instructions for the person who will be doing the work, and an estimate of the time involved.

This part of the planning process involves careful time management. Some steps can take place independently of others, but many will be linear and require one step to be completed before the next can begin. The same can be said of many tasks we undertake every day; we just are less formal in organizing them.

We need to drop off the dry cleaning before we can pick it up, of course, and we may need to research information before we write a report. If we stopped to consider how much time it will take to perform the research, we would have a better idea of how long it will take to produce the report.

Task Allocation

The next stage is allocating the steps of the project to individuals in the project team. This often requires a global view; the manager needs to be aware of outside demands on team members, and most importantly, to take advantage of individual strengths and build skills within the team for future projects. Tasks can be modified to fit the experience of individuals, and grouped if they have common requirements. Task allocation is an opportunity to develop the team as a collection of individuals.

Time management is task management, whether for a project or for your own individual tasks. By thoroughly understanding a task, you can allocate the appropriate resources and schedule it accurately. If you are working with your own personal set of skills, you should be realistic in understanding how to take advantage of your strengths and accommodate your weaknesses to accomplish your goals.

Time Estimating

We've already seen how by breaking down a project into manageable steps, it's possible to assign them a schedule. Then, by putting together the steps into the longest path, you can get a good idea of the total time the project will require. There are lots of assumptions to be made and time estimating can be a scary process.

It's important to keep records of how long individual activities take so you can use this experience in future projects.

If you don't have the results of previous projects to use in estimating the current one, then you're left with trying to guess time requirements as accurately as possible.

It's tempting to be optimistic, ignoring potential or unknown problems, and assuming things will go smoothly. Problems have been known to occur in the best planned project, so it's wise to build in some slack so it doesn't blow your schedule out of the water. Your superiors may encourage you to deliver faster, and there may be honest business reasons to do so, but resist the pressure to compromise quality or give unrealistic promises.

These principles apply equally to planning individual tasks. To successfully work your way through the day's to-do list, you need to know how much time each task will require, and be realistic in establishing your schedule. No matter how urgent they may be, or strong your desire to cross them off your list, you will not complete five three-hour tasks in an eight-hour day.

Managing The Project

Once the specifying, planning, task allocation, and time estimating is completed, its time to pull the trigger on your project. It will be necessary to apply controls to the project, despite its apparent willingness to take on a life of its own. Because you have created steps or stages for a complex project, you know what needs to be accomplished and by what date.

These milestones enable you to monitor progress (forming the basis for the popular "progress report") and serve as interim goals for the individuals or groups working assigned to them. Sometimes it's preferable to establish milestones that don't match the steps of the project, but recognize a particular achievement resulting from the completion of several steps.

Effective communication is a critical component of project management; it merits its own set of rules. The team must communicate with each other and their manager; if there are multiple teams, they must communicate with each other; and the project manager must communicate with senior management.

Communications permit you to monitor and report progress, encourage cooperation, and motivate. Any breakdown in communications within the project management team can spell disaster.

Monitoring progress through milestones, particularly tasks with multiple steps, is an equally effective technique on a personal level.

CHAPTER 15: LESSONS FROM THE POMODORO TECHNIQUE

I n the business market it's also recommended to use the Time Timer. Explore the Pomodoro technique. Focus on work for 25 minutes and then take a five minute break.

If you're like most people, time management can be a challenge. Odds are you're bombarded with work tasks, personal projects, lengthy to-do lists and constant emails flooding your inbox.

So, how do you get it all done in the most efficient manner?

One possible solution is to use a popular time blocking system called the Pomodoro Technique. I'll talk about how the 25-minute "Pomodoro habit" can help you quickly complete tasks and get things done in a streamlined fashion.

Why is Effective Time Management Important?

A few years back, I discovered a simple truth called Parkison's Law. It states:

Work expands so as to fill the time available for its completion.

Put succinctly, this rule means that the more time you "give" a project, the longer you'll take to complete it. Have a deadline a week from now? Odds are you'll take the full week to do it.

The best way to combat Parkinson's Law is to manufacture strict deadlines with yourself and to literally have a ticking clock in the background as you work on each task. Not only will this help you become more productive, you'll also "get more time" that can be spent doing the fun things in life.

Think of it this way:

There are only 675,450 hours in the average human life. Every hour that's wasted is an hour you won't get back. If you're working hard every day but not getting measurable results, then you're wasting your life—one hour at a time.

The solution is simple:

Stop randomly working on projects. Instead, create a plan for the important tasks and work on each with a completely focused mindset. And the best tool for doing this is through the Pomodoro Technique.

What is the Pomodoro Technique?

In the late 1980's, Francesco Cirillo first came up with the Pomodoro System. Cirillo came up with the name (which is an Italian word for "tomato") because he utilized a tomato-shaped egg timer when managing his time.

The idea behind the Pomodoro Technique is to break down all of your tasks into 25 minute time blocks. Between each time block, there is a five minute break. And after completing four Pomodoros you take a longer break— usually 15 to 30 minutes.

In theory, this strategy works because you completely focus on one task (like writing) without shifting focus or multitasking. When the clock is ticking, you ignore the urge to check email, hop on Facebook, answer text messages or do any other distracting activity. You're in the zone and completely focused.

If you decide to implement this system you'll be able to:

✓ Eliminate the multi-tasking habit.

✓ Focus on the task at hand.

✓ Get more things done because you'll have a sense of urgency.

✓ Avoid the perfectionist mindset by overly "fine-tuning" a project.

✓ Build higher levels of willpower and concentration.

✓ Decrease stress levels because you're doing one thing at a time.

That just a taste of what your life could be like by using the Pomodoro technique. So let's talk about to develop this time-blocking habit.

Pomodoro Technique in Five Simple Steps

Here's the recommended process for following the Pomodoro method:Pomodoro Technique - Time Blocking Method

✓ Choose your task and total time to work on it.

✓ Set a timer to 25 minutes (either with an egg timer or with an app).

✓ Work on the task for 25 minutes. Avoid all distractions and urges to multi-task.

✓ Take a 5-minute break for energy renewal, start another Pomodoro.

✓ Take a 20-30 minute break after completing four Pomodoros.

Simple, but very effective. When you use this technique you'll see a dramatic improvement in your productivity and ability to get things done.

Rules for the Pomodoro Technique

Like any system, there are rules to follow and rules to ignore. That's why I recommend my variation on the above system. Here are four guidelines that can maximize your results:

Breaks are NOT Optional

When that buzzer rings, stop work, get up and take a break. You need this time for your mind to relax and to get energized for that next task. Use it to: Do simple exercises, grab a snack, go to the restroom, stretch or make a cup of tea. It really doesn't matter what you do, just as long as you're taking a break.

Time Length = Challenge of Task

What I'm about to suggest breaks the primary rule of the Pomodoro Technique…so use it at your own discretion:

The way I use this method is to work in multiples of the 25-minute blocks.

The actual amount of time I spent fully-focused on a task depends on its level of difficulty. Easy tasks (i.e.; a low level of concentration) can be can be completed in 50-minute (2 Pomodoros) or 1 hour and 15-minute (3 Pomdoros) blocks of time. Harder tasks (i.e.; a high level of concentration) can be completed using the standard 25-minute block of time. Really the number of Pomodoros you do should relate to how long you can focus on a task without feeling distracted.

Batch Related Pomodoros

Tasks that take less than 25 minutes should be grouped together instead of being done separately.

For instance, I have a task that's labeled "communication," which includes talking to people through email, Twitter, Pinterest, Google+ and Facebook. Each site might only take five minutes of my time, so I've developed a system where I run a few back-to-back Pomodoros and go through all of them at once.

Benefits of the pomodoro technique

A deadline is never kind enough to allow you to deliver before the 11th hour.

There is even an adage for that! 'Work expands so as to fill the time available for its completion'? That there is Parkinson's law, it means that work contracts to fill the time you make for it. Sound familiar?

The pomodoro technique is a simple time management methodology that is an equal opponent to this adage. Discover the hidden benefits of the technique and how they will help you to understand;

✓ The value of your time.

✓ How you can improve the quality and quantity of your work.

✓ What you can do better to manage people's expectations, including your own!

✓ How exercising your willpower can benefit you.

✓ How you can stop fighting the clock.

✓ The best way to eliminate burnout.

Now is the time to learn more about what makes the pomodoro technique so effective at helping people to complete high-quality work productively.

Knowing your worth

Your time is valuable, whether you are charging for it or not.

 The pomodoro technique allows you to calculate the value of your time, plan your pomodoro sessions accordingly and then work to that plan to deliver a balanced outcome. Don't over deliver wasting time, and don't under-deliver because you didn't give yourself enough time.

The pomodoro technique is especially useful for people working on flat rate projects, to ensure they maintain a profitable hourly rate and equally useful as a method to fit everything into any busy life.

Planning the effort required for a job in pomodoro sessions will help you meet your timeframe and value targets, improving the bottom line and/or work/life balance.

Improving output

The pomodoro technique increases focus immensely when prescribed to correctly.

 In turn, this leads to an increase in work turnover and a boost in quality.

 Yep, that is right, more work, better quality, all with the same amount of hours in a day.

How is this possible? Simple, the pomdoro technique teaches us to focus. Firstly by prescribing that you pick one task to focus on per pomodoro session. Secondly by motivating you to manage distractions.

 Think about all the distractions you have in a day. We will happily abandon what we are working on to answer phone calls, emails or instant messages.

 By managing distractions to your advantage, you perform better, and the absolute worst that can happen is you might return a call, email or message 25 minutes later.

Managing expectations

As you now know, using the pomodoro technique you can more accurately estimate how long it will take you to complete tasks.

 The flow on from this is you can manage expectations better. Not just those of clients, teachers, teams or management, but also your own.

You will no longer kid yourself that you will be able to get a 10-hour job done in one day because you know 10 hours equates to 20+ pomodoro sessions and that, with a 5-minute break every 25 minutes and 20-minute break every four sessions, will never fit into your day alongside everything else.

Because you know this, you don't leave it until the last day or you don't tell your boss you can have it done by tomorrow.

Well managed expectations mean no frustration over missed deliveries.

Exercise your willpower

There are so many apps and tools out there that will shut out distractions for you, they will block you from visiting certain websites, they will play you white noise to help you concentrate and so much more.

But what about using your inner energy to work towards achieving your goals. To strengthen your resolve to get more done.

Exercise your will power to achieve focus and concentration. Choose to be productive.

Work with time

There is something unique about the pomodoro technique, something that people don't understand until they have used it. It is actually hard to explain too, but here goes.

When you use the pomdoro technique, you lose the feeling you are always fighting against time. There are a few reasons for this;

You become a pro at managing expectations and setting deadlines.

Time is broken into 25-minute chunks, so you tend to focus only on the present pomodoro session.

You feel less stressed because you cannot multi-task nor let interruptions take your attention.

I can't say it better than Sue Shellenbarger of the Wall Street Journal, "It eased my anxiety over the passing of time and also made me more efficient; refreshed by breaks, for example, I halved the total time required to fact-check a column."

Eliminate burnout

You have reached the end of your day and you are exhausted.

You feel like this every day, and you have no idea how anyone can avoid it. How can they have extra-curricular activities? How do they have energy?

You too can have this. You don't have to reach the end of your day with no capability to even think about having a conversation, let alone actually having a conversation!

The pomodoro technique is effective at keeping you fresh by taking breaks after each session.

Chris Winfield on The Startup on Medium knows what I am talking about, "Taking short, scheduled breaks while working eliminates the 'running on fumes' feeling you get when you push yourself too hard. It's impossible to overwork when you stick to the system."

Simple is best

The pomodoro technique is so simple some people find it laughable. But as the saying goes, sometimes simple is best. With many surprising benefits, people never expect the uplift in productivity they experience from the Pomodoro technique.

It is an effective way to achieve a balance between quantity and quality, and all you have to do is focus for 25 minutes at a time.

CHAPTER 16: REACHING FULL POTENTIAL

Why does it seem like time goes by so quickly? We start a week and before we know it, it's already the weekend. How can you make the best out of each and every day? I want you to be able to reach your fullest potential every single day. Even during the days where you relax and recharge, I want you to enjoy every moment.

When it comes to reaching your fullest potential every day, it's all about planning. If you're not a good planner, you'll have to start learning! Those who are good with time management and are organized usually experience a more productive day.

Let's look into the ways you can reach your fullest potential every day.

Focus on the big picture

"Keep your thoughts positive because your thoughts become your words. Keep your words positive because your words become your behavior. Keep your behavior positive because your behavior becomes your habits. Keep your habits positive because your habits become your values. Keep your values positive because your values become your destiny." -Mahatma Gandhi

Because we live in a society filled with so many distractions, we can easily get caught up with the stress and frustrations of life. Focus on the big picture. With so many distractions, it's so important for you to focus on what you want. What does the big picture look like to you? What are the goals that you want to accomplish? When it comes to reaching your potential every day, it's important for you to know what the big picture looks like.

Why do you do what you do? What is the reason you go to work or come home and provide dinner for your family? When you have purpose and reason in your life, you're more able to live out each day to your fullest potential. If you are able to see the big picture in your life, you don't have to just live day-to-day. When you know your purpose, you will be motivated to live each day to your fullest potential.

Plan!

"Living your life without a plan is like watching television with someone else holding the remote control." – Peter Turla

Planning how you want to spend each day is key to reaching your fullest potential each day. Without any planning, you will just get pushed around and have no direction in life. Reaching your potential every day is about planning your day in alignment with what matters to you. Focus on what is important in your life. Maybe it's providing for your family or spending quality time with your spouse. When you are able to live in alignment with that matters to you, you will be able to reach your fullest potential every day.

Plan your week every Sunday evening. That way, you'll be able to see your week's schedule before starting your week. Make sure to add when you plan to start working and end working into your schedule. It will be important for you to know when it's time to turn off work-mode and start spending quality time with your family. It's also important that when you plan your week, you are realistic with what you want to accomplish.

Set yourself up for success, not for failure. Create a to-do list for each day of the week on Sunday evening. Have about 4-5 tasks you want to accomplish each day. If you have a big project, you should only include 2-3 tasks for that day. An action that has helped me reach my potential each day is to check off each task once I complete it. It feels good knowing that at the end of the day, I was able to complete my to-do list. Remember, set yourself up for success! Make sure you reward yourself after a long day of being productive.

Positive Attitude

"Positive and negative thinking are both contagious." -Stephen Richards

When it comes to reaching your fullest potential every day, it's important to have a positive attitude. When you have a negative attitude, you start viewing yourself and your life as being negative. How can you possibly reach your fullest potential when you have a negative attitude about yourself? It's all about your perspective and how you view yourself and your life. In order to have a productive day, you must have a positive attitude. With a positive attitude, you'll be able to stay focused on what you want to accomplish every day.

Stay focused on the task at hand

"Productivity is never an accident. It is always the result of a commitment to excellence, inteligent planning and focused effort." -Paul J. Meyer

Staying focused takes discipline and commitment. With so many distractions, it's easy to get off track and not get anything done. That's why staying focused on what you need to get done is key in reaching your fullest potential. If you get distracted by your phone, make sure you put it on silent when you're trying to finish a task. Not only will you be more disciplined, but you'll also get a lot more done! Anything that distracts you from completing a task needs to be put away.

Have Goals!

"A goal properly set is halfway reached." -Zig Ziglar

If you want to reach your fullest potential each and every day, you need to have short and long term goals. Take a piece of paper and write down what you want to accomplish now and in the future. This goes back to planning. Have your goals and have deadlines. Then plan each and every day taking the necessary steps to accomplish your goals. It's all about setting goals and then following through.

Simplicity

"Free yourself from the complexities of your life! A life of simplicity and happiness awaits you." -Steve Maraboli

When you want to reach your fullest potential, simplify what needs to get done before the day starts. One routine that has helped me save time is picking out my outfit the night before. This way, I don't feel rushed in the morning. Simplify your morning routine. If you can find different ways to save time and make your life simpler, you'll be able to focus on reaching your fullest potential every day. When you are constantly all over the place and your life is far from being simple, you'll experience stress and frustration on a daily basis. Simplify your life!

Recharge

"Take time to recharge your batteries. It's hard to see where you're going when your lights are dim." -Robert H. Conelly

You can only reach your fullest potential if you take the time to recharge. When you are constantly working without any rest, you will eventually burn out. Taking the time to rest and rejuvenate your mind, body and soul will allow you to become re-energized for the next day. Use different strategies that help you relax. Try meditating or taking a yoga class.

It is not only important for you to recharge your mind– your body needs time to recharge too. Reaching your fullest potential every day can become stressful if you don't manage your time well and take the time to recharge.

Take a moment and think about what recharges you. Maybe it's spending some quality time with your spouse or taking a nice walk in the park. Whatever you decide to do, make sure you enjoy the process. It's easy for our minds to wonder, so when you're recharging, focus on recharging!

Enjoy each moment

"To get all there is out of living, we must employ our time wisely, never being in too much of a hurry to stop and sip life, but never losing our sense of the enormous value of a minute." -Robert Updefraff

With so much going on, it's easy to just go, go, go and not take the time to smell the flowers. Enjoy the moments you experience throughout each day. This will help you feel grateful and appreciative with what you have in your life. Enjoy the simple things like having a roof over your head and being able to afford food for your family. Although being productive is important, taking the time to enjoy each moment is important too.

<u>Other Tips</u>

Envision your ultimate life

What would your ultimate life be like? Where would you live, what would you do, what would you do with your days? Come up with a clear picture of this, and write it down. Now, one step at a time, make it come true. Some ways of doing that follow.

Set long-term goals

Your vision of your ultimate life will help you come up with long-term goals. Of those goals, pick one to accomplish within the next year, and really focus on that. Now, pick one medium-term goal to achieve in the next few months that will get you further toward your longer-term goal. Now decide what you can do this week, and today, to get you to your medium-term goal. Just choose one thing at a time, focus on it, make it happen, and then choose the next thing to focus on.

Review goals

Setting goals is important, but the key to making them a reality is actually reviewing them (at least monthly, but weekly is better) and taking action steps to make them come true. Again, focus on one at a time, and really focus on them.

Life mission

Related to envisioning your ultimate life, but different — it's important that you think about how you would like to be remembered when you die, so you can start living the life that leads to that now. Live with purpose in life, and wake up every day with that purpose in mind.

Plan your big tasks for week and day

Give purpose to your day by determining the three most important things you can do with your day, and making those a priority. Do the same thing with your week to increase your productivity: pick out the big tasks you'd like to accomplish this week, and schedule those first.

Maintain focus

One important key to achieving your goals is to maintain focus on them. To do this, again, it's important that you select one goal at a time. This will prevent your focus from spreading too thin. It's also important that you give yourself constant reminders of your goal, so you don't lose that focus. Put up a poster of your current goal, or print it out and put it out somewhere visible, and send yourself emailed reminders. However you do it, find a way to maintain a laser-sharp focus, and the goal will come true.

Enjoy the journey

Goals are important, but not at the expense of happiness now. It's important to maintain a balance between going where you want to go, and being happy as you go there. It's easy to forget that, so be sure to remind yourself of this little, but important, tip as you make your journey.

Create a morning and evening routine

These are two great ways to add structure to your day, make sure you review your goals and log your progress, and get your day off to a great start. An evening routine, for example, could be a great way not only to wind down from a long day and review how your day went, but to prepare yourself for your next day so the morning isn't so hectic. Your morning routine is great way to greet the day, to get some exercise or meditation or quiet contemplation, or to get some writing or other work done.

Try rising early

It's not for everyone, I'll admit. It may not be for you. But I've found it to be an amazing change in my life. It has made the start of my days much more positive, and I now have time for writing, exercise, and silent contemplation.

Do less

This is both a happiness and productivity tip. Doing less will make you happier, because your life won't be so hectic and filled with stress. You will have time for things that give you pleasure, for the loved ones in your life, for life itself. It's also a productivity tip: if you focus on the essential tasks, the big ones, the ones that will give you the most return for your time, and eliminate the rest, you will actually be more productive. You'll get fewer tasks done, but you will be more effective.

Exercise

Make this a daily habit. Exercise not only helps you lose weight, but for me, it's made me feel so much better. I actually enjoy exercise now. It's a time of contemplation for me, and I feel so much better about myself afterwards.

Eat healthy

I don't recommend dieting. It's too restrictive and you usually fall off it at some point. I do recommend changes to your diet, however — ones you make gradually, and that can be sustained for life. It not only helps lose weight, but really, once you start eating healthier, it is actually much more enjoyable.

Think positive

Another one of the most important tips on this list, thinking positive — as cliche as it might sound — is one of the single best changes you can make in your life that will lead to so many more positive tips. As I wrote about here, learning to think positive was the skill that turned my life around. It makes everything else on this list possible. Read more about it here.

Simplify your finances

Cut down on the number of accounts you have, cut down on your credit cards, spend less, reduce your bills. Make your finances automagical. Simplifying your finances greatly reduces your stress.

Simplify your life

Another of my top tips. I've greatly simplified my life, in many ways, and I can say that having less stuff in my life, and less to do, has greatly increased my enjoyment of life. De-clutter, simplify your commitments, simplify your work space, simplify your wardrobe, simplify your rooms.

Develop intimate relationships

It's great to have a special someone, of course, but intimate relationships could be found with anyone around you. If you have a significant other, be sure to spend time each day and each week with that person, to work on your relationship and communicate and continue to bond. But if you don't, there's no need to despair (if in fact you are) … intimate relationships can be developed with friends, other family members, kids, roommates, classmate, co-workers.

Every single person we meet is a fellow human being, with the same desires for happiness, for food and shelter, for an intimate connection. Find that common thread, be open and sincere, find out more about each other, understand each other, and give love. This can be one of the most important things you do.

Eliminate debt

Financially, this is a huge way to relieve stress and make you feel much more secure. I suggest that you get rid of your credit cards (if you have a problem with credit card debt or impulse spending) and create a snowball plan for yourself. It may take a couple of years, but you can get out of debt.

Empty your inbox and clear your desk

This might take a little while to do at first, but once you've emptied your inbox and cleared off your desk, it doesn't take long to keep them clear from then on. It's a simple habit that's vastly rewarding. I get an inordinate amount of pleasure from having a clean desk. I recommend you give it a try.

Limit your information intake

In our lives today, we get a tremendous amount of information through email, blog feeds, reading websites, paperwork, memos, newspapers, magazines, television, DVDs, radio, mobile phones and Blackberries. Not only can this be overwhelming, but it can be distracting and can fill up your life until you have no time for more important things. Go on a media fast to get control over your information intake, and to simplify your life

Create simple systems

Once you've simplified your life, the way to keep it simple is by creating systems for everything you do regularly. Create an efficient system for laundry, mail and paperwork, errands, your workflow. Anything, really. See ways to Streamline Your Life and to make your mail and paperwork painless.

Take time to decompress after stress

There will inevitably be times in your life when you go through high stress. Perhaps several times a week. To maintain your sanity, you need to find ways to decompress. Here are some great ways to do that.

Focus on benefits, not difficulties

If you find yourself struggling to do something, or procrastinating, stop thinking about how hard something is, or why you don't want to do it. Focus instead on what benefits it will have for you, what opportunities it will create — the good things about it. By changing the way you see things, you can change how you feel about them and make it easier to get things done.

Get into the flow

This is both a happiness and productivity tip. Flow is the term for the state we enter when we are completely focused on the work or task before us. We are so immersed in our task that we lose track of time. Having work and leisure that gets you in this state of flow will almost undoubtedly lead to happiness.

People find the greatest enjoyment not when they're passively mindless, but when they're absorbed in a mindful challenge. Get into that flow by first doing something you are passionate about, and second by eliminating all distractions and really focusing on the task before you.

Be frugal

This is a habit, rather than a goal. It is a way of living, a different mindset, and the best way to live within your means. It doesn't mean being cheap or forsaking pleasure, but it does mean finding less expensive ways to do things, learning to live with less (and be happier in the process), and controlling impulse spending.

Learn to deal with detractors

We all face detractors in our lives. They are the naysayers who, even if they are well-intentioned, will make us feel unworthy, or that you cannot achieve a goal. They will tease or be negative. In order to achieve your goals, you need to learn how to deal with these detractors and overcome this common obstacle.

Go outdoors

These days, too many of us spend so much of our time indoors, especially if our jobs and our ways of having fun are all online. Our kids are often just as bad or worse, with so many ways to watch TV, surf the Internet or play video games. Get them and yourself outdoors, appreciate nature, the beauty of the world around us, and the fun of physical activity. See this article for more ideas (to do with or without kids).

Retire early

This isn't a sure way to become happy — you can retire and be bored out of your mind and unhappy — but it's surely a cool goal. And if you do something meaningful with your life, such as volunteer and help others, it can be a way to be really happy. It's not an easy goal, either, but you can retire early by cutting back on your living expenses, increasing your income, and investing the difference. The more you can do of all three, the faster you'll retire. And that's a truly liberating idea.